There A  D0379779

"This is a must-read for people who are mourning the loss of their animal family . . . Comforting and compassionate . . . Sonya guides you to the understanding that the spirit lives on."

—John Edward

"When you have the privilege of knowing Sonya, as I have, believe me, there are no sad dogs in heaven."

—Robert Wagner

Praise for
Sonya Fitzpatrick

"*The Pet Psychic* opens a new door to the world of animal interaction."
—*News-Sun*

"A cat's-eye view of the world. Through cat tale after cat tale, she reveals what's most important to our feline companions and friends."
—*St. Louis Post-Dispatch*

"A modern-day Dr. Doolittle."
—WashingtonPost.com

continued . . .

There Are No
Sad Dogs in Heaven

Finding Comfort After the Loss of a Pet

SONYA FITZPATRICK

BERKLEY BOOKS, NEW YORK

THE BERKLEY PUBLISHING GROUP
Published by the Penguin Group
Penguin Group (USA)
375 Hudson Street, New York, New York 10014, USA

USA | Canada | UK | Ireland | Australia | New Zealand | India | South Africa | China

Penguin Books Ltd., Registered Offices: 80 Strand, London WC2R 0RL, England
For more information about the Penguin Group, visit penguin.com.

This book is an original publication of The Berkley Publishing Group.

THERE ARE NO SAD DOGS IN HEAVEN

An application to register this book for cataloging has been submitted to the Library of Congress.

PUBLISHING HISTORY
Berkley trade paperback edition / September 2013

ISBN: 978-0-425-26113-2

PRINTED IN THE UNITED STATES OF AMERICA

10 9 8 7 6 5 4 3 2 1

Cover design by Diana Kolsky
Cover photo: Dog and Cat © Ermolaev Alexander / Shutterstock
Book design by Laura K. Corless

To all my animals in the spiritual and physical realms,
who have given me so much joy.

My dogs in their physical bodies:
Sally, Moe, Jack, Joy, Lucky, and Maggie

My dogs in spirit:
Traybe, Sabrina, Silky, Brue, Bella, Ellie, Judy, Sam,
Foxie, Honey, and Holly

My cats in their physical bodies:
Sunshine, Polly I and Polly II, Molly, Clair,
Rosie, Dante, and Fudge

My cats in spirit:
Cinnamon, Raisin, Blackie, Moonbeam,
Wellington, Smokie, Jennie, Farmcat, Tiger, Cocoa,
Churchill, Winston, and Winnie

My horse in his physical body: Lucky

My horses in spirit: Blackie and Pickles

My childhood geese in spirit:
Buttercup, Daisy, and Primrose

My chickens in spirit:
Henrietta, Clover, Dowsey, and Chip Chip

ACKNOWLEDGMENTS

I would like to express my gratitude to all the people who were involved in making this book happen.

To Nancy Yost, my literary agent, for always believing in me.

To Judy Kern for her contribution to bringing this manuscript to a successful conclusion.

To Denise Silvestro, my editor at Berkley, for early support and continuing guidance.

For my devoted publicist, Brona Hanley, of Big Noise Productions.

To my daughter, Emma, for her loving support and the hard work she puts into acting as my personal assistant as well as for giving me my wonderful grandchildren, Emily and Peter.

To my sons, Sean and Patrick, for a unique relationship and for caring so much about the treatment of animals that they became vegans.

To my spirit guides, Dr. Thompson, Edgar Cayce, and Harry Edwards, and to my spiritual mentor, Saint Francis.

To all of my clients and their wonderful children in fur coats for making this book possible.

To the many sanctuaries and rescue organizations that have saved animals and changed their lives forever, including:

Best Friends Animal Sanctuary (www.bestfriends.org)
Houston BARC Foundation (www.houstonbarcfoundation.org)
Montgomery County Animal Shelter (www.mcaspets.org)
North Shore Animal League (www.animalleague.org)

Acknowledgments

Pets Alive Animal Sanctuary (www.petsalive.com)
Special Pals Animal Adoption Center (www.special
   palshouston.org)
World Wildlife Fund (www.worldwildlife.org)

CONTENTS

Contents

INTRODUCTION

Losing Ellie

I grew up on a farm in England where there were no other children to play with, and I also had a serious hearing loss that made it difficult for me to communicate with people. Perhaps for these reasons, I learned at a very early age that I was able to communicate with animals in a way most people could not. Animals communicate telepathically, with mental images and physical feelings that don't depend on hearing, so the farm animals became my best friends. Along with the joys of those friendships, however, came the deep pain and sorrow I felt whenever one of them was butchered or killed, as happens frequently on a farm.

I now live in Texas, in a house with a large garden, surrounded by numerous dogs and cats of all varieties, and I spend virtually every day assuring clients who both book telephone readings with me and those who call in to my Sirius radio program, "Animal Intuition," that animals live on in spirit, just as people do, after they've passed from our lives. But I still feel the same heartbreak they do when one of my own beloved animals leaves me.

Perhaps the most profound pain I've ever felt at the loss of a pet came when I knew my dear Ellie, a Rhodesian ridgeback, was nearing the end of her life on earth. I love all my animals, of course, but Ellie and I seemed to have an especially deep soul connection. For thirteen years I had cried into Ellie's neck when I was sad and shared my joys and triumphs with her, but now I could tell that her back legs were getting weak and achy, and then, one day, she suddenly became very ill.

I had been walking in the woods near my home with her and the other dogs, as we did every day, when Ellie suddenly fell to the ground and rolled on her side, unable to get up. I collapsed to the ground next to her and held her head in my arms as she looked deeply into my eyes. Ellie weighed one hundred twenty-five pounds and I knew there was no way I'd be able to carry her the half mile out of the woods and back to the road. At that point I was absolutely frantic. The last thing I wanted to do was leave her there alone, but I knew that if I didn't get help quickly she would die. I know she understood me when I told her telepathically that I would have to leave her for a little while but that I'd be back as quickly as possible. Then I picked up my two small dogs, called to the third to follow me, and ran as quickly as I could, tears streaming down my face, exhorting my spirit guides to bring the help I needed.

As I emerged from the trees, miraculously there was a truck coming down the road toward me. Frantically I waved it down, breathlessly explained to the driver that my dog had collapsed in the woods, and begged him to help me carry her out. Seeing how upset I was, he immediately said that he lived nearby and urged me to get back to Ellie while he went to fetch the wheel-barrow from his garden so that we could transport her to my car.

Then, taking the other dogs with him so that I wouldn't have to worry about them, he drove off as I raced back into the woods. I could sense that Ellie was still in her body, and as I ran I sent her telepathic messages begging her to wait for me. As I dropped to the ground and once more took her head in my arms, she turned to look at me. I put my hands on her and asked God and my spirit guides to send healing energy into her body while also letting her know that if she needed to pass over into the spirit realm it would be okay for her to leave. Doing that was very painful for me, but I knew that, because our bond was so strong, she needed to have my permission to go. Animals are willing and able to endure a lot of pain when they feel they need to stay in their physical bodies because their human companion isn't ready to let them go.

Ellie didn't die that day, but I knew that the time she had left in her physical body would be short. After doing some tests, the vet told me that she had Addison's disease, which causes the slow deterioration of the adrenal gland, and that she had suffered an Addison's crisis brought on by elevated levels of potassium, which cause a disruption of the heart rhythm and a drop in blood pressure. Because the symptoms of Addison's are vague, generally presenting primarily as weakness or listlessness, I had attributed Ellie's decrease in energy to her age. The average life span of a ridgeback is about ten years, and Ellie was already thirteen.

She was put on an IV drip, and after three days I was able to bring her home. She was still very weak, however, and unable to jump up on my bed, where she had slept every night since she came to live with me. So I went out and bought the biggest dog bed I could find and then wound up sleeping on the floor next to her with my arm flung over her back.

I kept reassuring her, both aloud and telepathically, that this sort of thing happened to people as well, that we all got sick at one time or another. Apparently she thought this was very amusing because she cheekily asked me telepathically if it had ever happened to me. When I told her, "Not yet, but it could!" she laughed. Her body may have been weak but her sense of humor and her spirit were still strong.

For the next three days, I tempted her with everything I could think of to get her to eat—ice cream, baby food, cheese, yogurt, pureed chicken and vegetables—to help her get some strength back. Despite my best efforts, however, she couldn't eat more than a few bites at a time, and seeing her so ill was also making my other dogs very sad. They knew she was about to cross over and stayed very close to her, grieving her imminent loss.

Finally, on the fourth morning, I woke up next to her on the floor to find her panting. Her body was very hot, and I knew she was having another Addison's crisis. My daughter and ex-husband, who both live nearby, came immediately and helped me get Ellie into the car and to the emergency vet. As I climbed into the backseat with her, all I wanted was for her to be free of pain. Terrible as it would be for me to let her go, I knew that it was her time and that she would soon be returning to the spiritual realm.

As the vet made her comfortable, I put my head close to hers. I could sense that she was at peace. When he left me and my daughter, Emma, alone with her, I could see a beautiful white light surrounding us all. Then Ellie began to speak to me telepathically. *My time is very near,* she told me. *I am happy to be leaving my physical body, which is no longer able to function, but I will always be with you.* As she told me that, tears were actually running from her eyes, streaming down her face and onto my hands. I'd never seen anything like it before. And then I could feel the strength leaving her body. She was giving us her strength so that we could bear the pain and grief of her passing. As Emma and I each put one hand on Ellie and joined our other hands together, we felt an enormous sense of love and peace come over us. She was an exceptional soul and very enlightened. She was very aware that she was on her way back to the spiritual realm.

Ellie told me that she would always be with me. Then she asked me to leave so that she could pass over. For the last time, I looked into her deep brown eyes and kissed her goodbye. I knew that my leaving would be the last gift of grace I could give her. I knew she wanted me to be happy because she was passing into a beautiful place, and I knew our souls would meet again, but that didn't make it any less painful for me to be losing her physical presence.

When Emma and I arrived home, all the other animals were gathered at the door to greet us. We huddled together until, at precisely three-thirty that afternoon, we all felt Ellie leave her body. In that moment, the sense of her presence was overwhelming. The room filled with a spiritual light and in my mind's eye I could see all the animals with whom I'd been privileged to share my life in the past gather around her on the other side. Then the telephone rang. It was the veterinarian calling to tell me that Ellie was gone. But I knew she wasn't gone. She was right there with me. I could feel her head resting on my knee on the sofa, and the other dogs spontaneously moved over to make room for her next to me.

I tell you this story for two reasons: to let you know that I fully understand and empathize with whatever pain and sorrow you may have felt at losing a beloved animal companion, and also to reassure you that your pet is still very much with you in the world of spirit. In the pages that follow, you will read the stories of many other people I have helped come to this understanding, and I profoundly wish that, as a result, you will feel the same sense of comfort, even in your grief, that I was able to bring them. As I provide answers to their questions, I hope that they will answer many of yours as well.

ONE

Where Is My Pet Now?

It was just days after Cleo died, and Maggie could hardly say her much-loved Welsh corgi's name without bursting into tears. She had booked a telephone reading with me, and, between sobs, she explained that her house felt very empty now but also that she sometimes imagined she could feel Cleo's weight on her lap or pressing against her leg. She was afraid she might actually be losing her mind. *Where is Cleo now?* Maggie whispered. *Is she with other animals? Is there a special place animals go after they die?* She had known for some time that Cleo was coming to the end of their time together. She'd lived a long, full life and went peacefully in Maggie's arms, but Maggie had not yet made peace with her passing. She needed to be assured that the dog she had raised from puppyhood was happy in the world of spirit, and that she wasn't lonely.

This is one of the first questions most people ask me, and I'm happy to be able to put their minds at rest. Cleo came through to me almost immediately, and I told Maggie that I could see her—in my mind's eye, of course. What happens is that I get a mental image, much the same way as, if I asked you a question about the Statue of Liberty you would immediately get a mental picture of the statue. Cleo was showing me a fuzzy, if somewhat battered, green frog, and she was surrounded by several other animals as well as a group of people. *Oh,* Maggie sobbed, *that was her favorite toy. She had it for years! And I'm so glad she's not alone. She hated being left alone.*

I assured her that Cleo was not alone, and neither was she. Maggie wasn't going crazy and she wasn't imagining Cleo's continued presence in her life. I then explained to her that our animals go to the same world of spirit we do. There is no separate place for animals, and our souls will be reunited once we, too, pass into the spirit realm. In addition, you can rest assured that your animal never crosses over alone. He is usually met by another pet or human he has known on this plane or in a past life, and who has made the journey before him.

Maggie was comforted not only by the knowledge that Cleo was still able to communicate with her but also by the fact that she was surrounded by old friends. This is one of the most reassuring messages I can give to the grieving clients I speak with every day.

Cows Go to Heaven, Too

Elena and her daughter, Heather, are devout animal lovers.

Elena's father was a dairy farmer. He had nine cows and two goats, Sissy and Sadie, and when he died, Elena promised the cows that she would never allow them to be slaughtered. She found a small house in the country, many miles from the nearest town, with six acres of land, which was enough for her to keep the cows. Unfortunately, however, the house had been abandoned for several years and was in a state of disrepair when she bought it. Elena wasn't young anymore, and keeping up with the maintenance, both physically and in terms of the cost, was difficult for her.

Still, she struggled on until one day, when she was in the pasture feeding the cows their favorite treat, which happened to be bananas, one of them accidentally bumped into her and knocked her over. Elena struggled to get back on her feet and eventually got herself back to the house and called her daughter. Heather, of course, was upset and very worried. She told Elena that she really couldn't continue to live out there on her own. It was just too isolated and too dangerous.

But Elena wouldn't leave until she'd found a good home for the cows. Both Elena and Heather had been longtime clients, so when she called me I said I'd see what I could do to help her out. I phoned another one of my clients who has a large ranch with lots of animals. She said she couldn't take the cows but might know someone who could. A few days later, she called me with a phone number and said that a friend who had a ranch near hers would take the cows. I was really happy to deliver the good news to Elena, but she wasn't thrilled. She thought the ranch was too far away for her to be able to visit. So I said I'd keep looking.

A week later, I was out to dinner with my friends Dan and Helen, and I figured *Well, you never know, I might as well ask.* So I explained Elena's plight, and Helen immediately said that Cliff, who is Dan's partner in his medical practice, had a lot of land, was always taking in rescue animals, and could probably take the cows. I couldn't believe it. In two weeks I'd found two homes for nine cows. It seemed to be easier to find cows a home than it was to find a home for a dog or cat.

The day of the move finally arrived. When the wranglers came to get the cows into the trailer Elena absolutely refused to let them poke or prod the animals. She was holding a big stick and told the guys in no uncertain terms that if they poked her cows she'd be poking them. *Just ask them nicely,* she said. *They'll understand. They're very intelligent.* I was on the phone with Elena while this was going on, and I tuned in to the cows and explained telepathically that they were going to a new place that was very beautiful, that the people there would be taking good care of them, and that Elena would be coming to visit them often.

When they arrived they went to a beautiful pasture, and they communicated to me that they had loved the trip. Their new caretakers had ducks and geese, turtles and horses, potbellied pigs, and even a llama, all of which were rescues. But they also bred and slaughtered their own free-range cows, and that upset Elena very much. I understood her feelings, but I said, *Elena, that's just their way of life. They're meat eaters, but your cows are not going to be slaughtered.*

The cows settled in, and they loved their new home. Elena booked monthly telephone appointments with me so that I could communicate with them, and after a while I could feel that one of them, Mahogany, was having bladder problems. When an animal is sick, I feel in my own body where their illness or discomfort is located. Elena called the vet, and after he examined Mahogany he told Elena that she was suffering and her time had come. I got a mental image of another cow in spirit who'd been in Elena's herd and passed a few years before and was now coming to take Mahogany over. I knew that Mahogany could see her, too. And when I explained this to Elena, it made her feel a bit better.

Larry and John, who managed the ranch, dug Mahogany a grave in the pasture, and the next day the vet came to put her to sleep. Mahogany was at peace with her passing because I'd already explained to her that she'd be going back to the spirit world. I said that our physical body is just the vehicle we travel in when we're on earth and that when the body dies, we all go home to the spirit world, where we're all reunited with people we've known and loved in this and other lifetimes. I told her she'd be back with all the friends she'd known in this lifetime and other lifetimes when she wasn't a cow and that she'd be out of pain and full of joy. She was so calm, and so were all the other cows on the ranch.

Afterward, they all gathered around the grave and had a little service for her. The cows were sad because they'd miss her physical body, but I explained to them again that while this is our home for a while, we then all go to a special place where there's just peace and love and no pain. They were still sad, but they stood there while Larry and John filled Mahogany's grave and then they quietly walked away. Elena said it was a beautiful moment and she knew the cows understood that Mahogany was in a good place and was at peace.

Now, every time I do a reading for Elena, Mahogany comes through. She tells me all about what the other cows on the ranch are doing and gives me messages for them. They know she's around because they can feel her presence. Elena is thinking of putting a trailer on Cliff's land so that she can spend a few days at a time with her cow friends.

I continue to feel fortunate that I know so many people who dedicate their lives to helping animals and who understand that all animals have a soul and a consciousness.

We're All Together in the World of Spirit

Jan called me because her ten-year-old cat, Hattie, had been hit by a car and killed instantly. Jan was not only bereft, but also feeling terribly guilty because she believed it was her fault. She had three cats, and she told me that she always let them out in the mornings and got them back in before she left for work. On this particular morning, however, Hattie didn't come when she was called. Jan was in a hurry and because it was a nice day she assumed that Hattie would be okay. But Hattie apparently tried to cross the road and was run over.

Not only was Jan devastated, but also her two remaining cats, Ginger and Whisky, were sad and confused. They were grieving because they could feel Hattie's presence around them but they couldn't see her physical body. I explained to them that she had "gone home" to the place we all go when we leave our physical body, and that even though her body wasn't there anymore, she was still with them. They told me that their mother was very sad, and so were they.

I then explained to Jan that she had no reason to feel guilty about Hattie's death. It was Hattie's time, I told her, and there was nothing she could have done to change that.

As I was saying all this I could feel Hattie coming in, and

as she came closer I could see that someone was holding her. *Jan,* I said, *there's a woman holding Hattie. She was probably in her sixties when she died and she's telling me that she was very close to you.* Jan said that her mother had died in her sixties, and I told her that her mom was saying, *"From your arms to mine."* Jan was still crying but she said, *Oh, Sonya, that makes me so happy, because Hattie was my mother's cat and I took her when Mom died. Now they're back together again.*

At that point I could see that there was also a ginger colored cat with Jan's mother, and Jan told me that she'd had that cat for years. There was also a black-and-white one that had died of kidney failure that Jan told me had been her cat when she was a little girl. The cat was saying that she'd taught Jan everything she knew about animals, and Jan agreed that was correct. *She absolutely did,* Jan said. *It's from her that I got my love of cats.*

Well, I said, *you should know that they all come and sleep in your bed at night. Your bed is very full. And your living cats know that the others are there.*

At that point Jan's mother came back in and asked me to tell her daughter that her sofa looked very nice. Jan, who had recently had her sofa recovered, was absolutely amazed. *It looks much better,* her mother went on. *She sits on that couch every morning while she has her coffee. Please tell her I'll come to visit her while she's sitting there and I'll bring the cats with me.*

Jan was laughing and crying at the same time. *Tell her I'm so happy,* she said. *I've always believed people didn't just die, and*

I've often felt my mom around me. I'm going to sit on that sofa with my cats every morning, and I'm going to do the same thing every night right before I put out the light.

Where Is Buck Now?

Tom, a long-distance truck driver, phoned in to my radio show. Actually, I've found that I get many calls from truckers who are on the road for long periods of time and who often travel with their dogs.

Tom told me that he had his dog, Rosie, in the truck with him, but he wanted to know if I could contact another dog in spirit that he'd had as a boy. I told him I'd try and that animals usually do come through for me. And then I immediately got an image of a medium-size brown dog with a big white patch on his chest. *That's him,* Tom said, and I could hear the excitement in his voice. *That's my Buck. How is he over there?*

Well, I said, *just like all of them, he's at peace and full of love, and he visits with you still.*

Tom's voice broke then, as he said, *Tell him that I think of him every day of my life. I was fourteen years old when he passed, and he was the only one who ever gave me love in my young life.*

Well, Tom, I said, *he's telling me that he's with you every day and he rides in the truck with you. Spirit brought him into your life and he's been with you in both animal and human form in many past lives. Also, you have been a dog in a past life, and you've been with him before.*

Thank you for telling me that, Sonya, he said. *I hope we had better lives in the past than we had in this one.* And then he said, *Tell him thank you for all the love he gave me. He licked my wounds on many occasions back then. He was my world, and he saved me, because there were many days when I don't think I could have gone on without him. But the thought of him having to live without me is what kept me going.*

Just to hear him say that almost broke my heart. Something about Tom really touched me deeply, and I asked him to e-mail me his phone number so that we could talk privately.

When he called for the reading we'd set up, he was just so excited and grateful. He said that he hadn't been able to sleep the night before, and that having this reading with me was like a dream come true. So I told him that I was going to talk to Rosie. *She's very happy,* I said, *and she's asking me if I'm a dog. I'm telling her that I'm a dog right now but I'm also a human. I'm telling her that the animals taught me their language, and that when I was young, I couldn't hear people talking because I was deaf, but I could always hear the animals, and I preferred talking to animals.*

Then Rosie came in and told me how happy she was living with Tom and that he'd rescued her from a shelter when she was about to be put to sleep. *That's true,* he said. *I walked into the shelter and asked them to show me the dogs that were about to be put down. I wanted to take them all. It really broke my heart. But this one came up to me and licked my hand, and I knew she was the one for me.*

She's telling me that she loves hamburgers and fish, I said. *And when you stop for food at one of those junk places you go to she always shares with you. She sleeps with you in the truck on a brown blanket. And she also says that you never leave her alone.*

That's absolutely right, he said. *Since the day I got her I will never leave her.*

Well, I said, *she's really happy.*

And that makes me happy, Tom said. *Tell her that, please.*

And then I could see that Buck was coming through again. *Tom,* I said. *Buck's here, and he's talking to me.* I could feel that he was a very special soul, and he told me that he'd been sent into Tom's life from spirit to be his angel and to help him. I could feel from him all the misery and confusion Tom had endured in his young years. And then I said, *Tom, he's telling me that you and he used to go to a store in the town where you lived.* And Tom said, *Yes. I used to work for the storekeeper, and he was a very kind man. He used to feed both me and Buck when sometimes we weren't being fed at home.*

Then Buck also told me that sometimes Tom was made to sleep in the barn and that Buck slept there with him and licked his face. *He did,* Tom said. *It was as if he were kissing me, and we used to keep each other warm.*

I knew he'd had a terrible life as a child, and I said, *You know, Tom, we're so much more than a physical body.*

— 17 —

I know that now, he said, *but as a kid you don't know that. I never learned anything about love from my family. When I found Buck, he became my family and he taught me how to love.* I could only think that, based on the loving energy I could feel coming from him through the phone line, Buck had taught him well.

Well, Tom, I said, *sometimes we have that special connection because our souls have been together in the past. And Buck wants you to know that he still sleeps on your bed every night watching over you. He's still your guardian angel.* And Tom said he knew that; he could feel it.

Animal Enlightenment

Jeff is a professional cyclist who has even competed in the Tour de France. He and his wife, Emily, are also Buddhists and practice meditation on a regular basis. I'd spoken with him many times because he and Emily had two ridgebacks whom they loved very much. Originally bred to fight lions in Africa, ridgebacks are extremely tenacious, and many have died because they simply wouldn't give up the fight. They are also extremely loyal and protective of their families. They don't bark unless they sense danger, and you can always trust their instincts. But they also love luxury, and you can often find them lounging on your bed or the most comfortable sofa.

I've had many ridgebacks myself, so I know them well and they hold a very special place in my heart. One of my ridgebacks would jump up on a chair, plant her backside, and sit with her feet in front of her just like a person whenever I took her to the vet. Needless to say, this always gave the other people in the waiting room a good laugh. She would also join us at the dining room table and we'd include her in the conversation. Jeff told me that his ridgebacks were human, and I agreed that no ridgeback I'd ever known had thought it was a dog.

Jeff often rode his bike through the countryside near his home, and one day, as he was peddling along a country road, two dogs ran out from a yard and one of them knocked him off his bike. Fortunately he wasn't hurt, but as he was picking himself up a truck came speeding down the other side of the road and hit one of the dogs. The other dog ran off home and the truck driver just kept going. Jeff went over to the injured dog and saw that he was badly hurt and also that he appeared to be part ridgeback. Not knowing what else to do, he carried the dog off to the side of the road so that he wouldn't be hit again and then walked back to the house the dogs had come from to inform the owner what had happened.

He knocked on the door and a woman answered. He told her what had happened and said that the dog needed to go to the vet because he was badly injured. *I'll take care of it,* she said, and shut the door in his face. So Jeff went back and waited with the dog, but when, after fifteen minutes, the woman still hadn't appeared, he went back and knocked again. This time, instead of opening the door she just shouted *Mind your own business and get off my property. I don't have money for a vet and anyway it's his fault for running into the road.* So once again Jeff went back to the dog, and this time he called his wife on his cell phone and told her to come with the van and bring a blanket because there was an injured dog they had to take to the vet. He then called the vet, who also happened to be a friend, and told him he was bringing in an injured dog. When Emily arrived, she and Jeff got both the dog and Jeff's bicycle into the van and were just about to drive away when Jeff saw a man carrying a shotgun coming out of the house where the dog lived. Jeff knew the man was going to shoot the dog, but, luckily, they were already in the van and just drove off down the road. He was also concerned about what would happen to the other dog, but he knew there was nothing he could do about it in that moment. The injured dog was his first concern.

The vet examined the dog and told Jeff and Emily that his leg was completely shattered and couldn't be saved. It would have to be amputated. Jeff and Emily were upset about that, but the vet assured them that the dog was young, just about two years old, had a lot of energy, and once he healed he'd be running around on his three legs just as fast as their other dogs. *But,* the vet said, *I can put him down if that's what you want me to do.*

Jeff and Emily told him to do the surgery, and the vet said that while he was at it he'd also neuter the dog and give him an identity chip. As the vet had predicted, the dog recovered nicely. Jeff and Emily named him Jack and took him home with them. For the first time, Jack had a family who loved and cared for him, and he also got along well with the other dogs. Within a couple of months, as the vet had predicted, he was doing just as well with three legs as they did with four. But Jeff and Emily still couldn't stop worrying about the other dog that had been left behind.

One day, they put Jack in the back of the van and drove out into the country. As they were passing the house where Jack had lived, true to form, the other dog ran out and started to chase the car. Jeff drove slowly down the road for about a mile and the dog was still following him. At that point Jeff stopped the car, opened the back, and led Jack out on his leash. The two dogs recognized each other immediately and had a joyful reunion. Jeff put them both in the van and drove immediately to the vet to have him checked out and neutered. While they certainly knew that, legally, they had kidnapped the second dog, Jeff and Emily always looked upon what they'd done as performing a rescue.

Over the years Jeff and Emily continued to call me. They were devoted to all their dogs and knew that they had all been together in many past lives. They meditated every day with their dogs, a custom that is not uncommon in Eastern cultures, and dogs, being metaphysical creatures, seem to understand it.

Finally the time came when Jack became very ill with Addison's disease and Jeff and Emily knew he would have to pass over. Jack understood that, as dogs do, and because they are so spiritually evolved, Jeff and Emily told me that they would be happy for Jack when his soul returned to the spirit world. Jeff asked me to tell him that they would meet with him each day in meditation, and that they were joyful for him.

Jack passed out of his body very easily. When Jeff and Emily booked an appointment with me to talk with him, Jack told me that he'd been at home with them and they had talked him through his passing. He said that he had felt no fear. He could hear them talking to him, and he also wanted me to tell them how happy he'd been with them in this lifetime.

Then I could also feel the other dogs' presence, and I knew that they were at peace about Jack's passing. Because Emily and Jeff were so enlightened, the animals that came into their lives also became enlightened. They knew that Jack was happy in the spirit world and also that he was still with them.

TWO

Is My Animal Happy?
Does He Miss Me?
What Is He Doing Now?

One reason Julie was having such a hard time getting over the death of her longtime poodle companion, Sugar, was that Sugar had always suffered from terrible separation anxiety. *She always got so upset when I left her,* Julie said. *It just broke my heart to think that she could doubt even for a moment that I would be coming back to her. I always told her where I was going and when I'd be returning, and I know she understood me. She was so smart. She understood everything. But she just couldn't help worrying. And each time I came back she would whirl and twirl in front of me as if she just couldn't contain her joy and surprise that I'd actually kept my promise. Now that she's gone I can finally understand how she felt.*

I'm missing her so much that I can't believe she isn't missing me, too, and I just need to know that she's happy wherever she is.

In my mind, I could see that Sugar was right there next to Julie all the while Julie was talking with me on the phone. I could see her impish little face, and I could hear her laughing. *Doesn't she know I'm with her all the time now?* Sugar asked. *I did miss her when she left me alone, but now I can go with her everywhere, so I don't have to have that anxiety anymore. And I'm never alone. Please let her know that I'm very happy and I want her to be happy, too. Tell her that she can talk to me whenever she wants. I'm only a thought away!*

When I conveyed Sugar's message to Julie, she burst into tears, but they were tears of joy and relief. What I want everyone to know is that our animals are always happy in the spirit world. It's a place where there is no sadness, no loneliness, no fear. And they don't have to miss us because they remain with us even when they are no longer in their physical bodies. They can come to us whenever they want, even sleep with us in their usual place on the bed. And if we let them know that we miss them, they will come and give us a sign that they're right there. Sometimes they even visit us in our dreams—we just need to be open and receptive to their presence. And in many cases they will actually reincarnate to be with us again in a physical body.

Emily's Gift

My granddaughter, Emily, was born with the same gift I have and could communicate with animals even before she could speak. When she was ten years old all she wanted was to take riding lessons. Courtney, the daughter of a close friend of mine, had just opened a stable, and I gave Emily lessons with her as a birthday present. The first horse Emily ever rode was called Graham. He was a beautiful older horse who was very reliable and loved to have children ride him. Emily felt completely at home in the saddle and was able to communicate with Graham telepathically.

She told me that she knew she had been with Graham in another life, and he knew it, too. *When I ride him,* she said, *I can tell how happy he is, and he tells me that he loves what he does. He's such a big horse, and he's so gentle. I always feel safe with him, and he tells me that he takes care of all the children who ride him.*

Emily always stays with me on Friday nights, and one Friday when she arrived she was very upset. *Graham isn't well, Grandma,* she said. *He isn't eating. Please tell him that he has to eat. I told him he had to eat, but I felt that he didn't want to eat. He wasn't hungry.*

As soon as I tuned in to Graham I could tell that something

was very wrong. I explained to Emily that he was old and that one day he would pass over.

Do you think that will happen now, Grandma? she asked.

I don't know, I said, *but if he doesn't get better and his time has come, he'll just go back to the spiritual realm. You know that's where he'll go, and you know he'll be very happy there.*

I also explained that Graham didn't want to eat because he wasn't feeling well, and if a horse doesn't want to eat you can't make him. Sometimes when people are sick they don't want to eat, and animals are very similar in that way.

A couple of weeks later, Graham died. Emily was devastated and told me that she missed him very much. *I do know he's gone home to the spirit world, and I feel that he's happy,* she said, *but I do miss him.*

I reminded her that she could still talk to him anytime she wanted because animals communicate telepathically exactly the same way when they're in the spiritual world as they do when they're in their bodies. *Sometimes,* I said, *when I'm talking to a client and I tune in to an animal, I'm not sure if they're in the spirit realm or here because they're still around and still talking and it's not always easy to know where they're coming from.*

I'm learning to live without him being in his physical body, Emily said. *And I will talk to him, Grandma. I do have these feelings of happiness, and I do feel that he's now at peace and out of pain.*

Well, you know that's how it is in the spiritual world, I said, and she agreed that she did.

A few weeks later Emily ran into my house bursting with joy. *Grandma,* she practically shouted, *I was on the school bus today and I looked out the window and guess what I saw.* I smiled, because I knew exactly what she'd seen. *It was Graham! I looked out the window and there he was, cantering along by the side of the bus. He was letting me know that he was still around me, and he looked beautiful! There was a white light all around him, and the pain of losing him just left me. I knew he was happy. I could feel it. And that made me happy, too.*

Since then she's told me that she still sees him from time to time when she's looking out the window on the bus. *Not every time,* she says, *but sometimes I do.*

When Birds Fly Free

David and John lived in a spacious loft in New York City that they had adapted to provide the best possible atmosphere for their two macaws, Rhett and Scarlett. The birds flew all over the apartment and David and John had hung swings, brought in eucalyptus trees, and created a mini-waterfall to make the environment as bird-friendly as possible. They'd also enclosed a portion of their large terrace so that Rhett and Scarlett could fly outside when the weather was warm enough. David and John didn't even take vacations because they didn't want to be away from their birds, and in their wills they had left both the loft and the birds to John's nephew.

David and John booked an appointment with me because they had noticed that Rhett seemed lethargic at times. They were worried about his health and were hoping I could find out what was wrong with him. When I tuned in to the birds, they were extremely eager to talk and tell me all about their lives. They told me that David and John also had a small dog named Bonnie that they liked very much. And Scarlett told me that her dads were always playing music by some famous singer— the guys said it was Elton John—and she said she thought the dog's bark sounded better. Both birds also told me that they had famous names, and they were very proud of that. One thing they didn't like, however, was sour grapes. They asked me to tell their dads to please taste the grapes first, because they threw the sour ones on the floor and even the dog wouldn't eat them.

Finally, Rhett told me that he wasn't eating much anyway because he wasn't feeling well. I could feel that something was affecting my nose, and I asked John and David what kind of cleaning products they used. They said that they used a professional cleaning company, and, in fact, they could smell the chemicals when the cleaning crew was done. *Unfortunately,* I said, *those chemicals are toxic, particularly to small animals. But,* I added, *I think there's also something else.*

At that point the birds sent me a mental picture of a new carpet. *John,* I said, *have you put down a new carpet? And how is it installed?* As it turned out, they'd recently laid sisal carpet-ing throughout the loft and anchored it with some kind of glue. They agreed that it had smelled terrible for about a week, par-ticularly since it was winter and they weren't able to open the windows. But then the odor had dissipated and they didn't think any more of it. *But that was really the last straw,* I said. *It's just too much for Rhett's and Scarlett's little bodies to absorb. I feel in my body that they're both very ill, probably more so than you think. You really need to get them both to a vet as quickly as possible, because the next thing to happen will be that they'll try to fly and won't be able to.*

Oh, Sonya, David said, *that's already happening to Rhett.*

When I heard that I really feared it was too late, and, in fact, they called me about a month later to say that they'd taken the birds out of the apartment, but they had both died—Rhett first and Scarlett a couple of weeks later. John and David were completely heartbroken. Here they'd thought they were doing everything possible to give their feathered children a good life, and all the while they'd unknowingly been contributing to their death.

As we were talking, the birds started to come through from the spirit world. I could see that they were with a very attractive lady who I felt had died of cancer. *Oh,* John said, *that's my mother. She died about five years ago.*

Well, I told him, *she's got Rhett on one shoulder and Scarlett on the other.* I could also see that she was very glamorous. *She's dressed in a very elegant black gown,* I told John, *and she's wearing pearls. She's very happy over there.* I could see that the birds had beautiful bright yellow and red feathers, and they just looked so right on her shoulders. *I wear them well, don't I,* she said, and John laughed. *That's my mother,* he said. *She was always perfectly dressed and groomed.*

And why am I hearing someone playing the piano? I asked. So he told me that his mother had been a professional pianist.

Well, I said, *she's telling me that they're with her and they're happy. And she wants you to know that there was nothing you could have done to prevent what happened because their time on the physical plane was up.*

John and David still didn't understand why the birds had to leave them, so I explained again that there was simply no answer to that for anyone, including us humans. At that point I could see that John's mother had been joined by a man who was telling me that he was John's father and he wanted John to know that he was sorry. *But,* I said to John, *it's not about the birds. He's sorry about something else.*

John then explained that when he'd told his parents he was gay, his father had basically cut him out of his life. *Well,* I said, *he's truly sorry about that now and he wants to know if you can forgive him.* John said that if his father was truly sorry, he would forgive him. Then he said, *It's the birds who've done this. They brought my father through, and they've helped me to forgive him. Thank you so much for doing this!*

I told him it wasn't me; it was Rhett and Scarlett. And I've found that very often, when something tragic happens, it happens for a reason. Our animals don't die in vain, and often they are able to help us. *Well,* John said, laughing, *I didn't think you'd be communicating with people!* I said that once I'd opened the door I never knew who was going to come through, and I assured him again that the birds' time on the earth plane had been over, and that, sad as it might have been, some good had come out of it.

Some time after, I got an e-mail from John and David telling me that they had called in a company to remediate the toxic chemicals in their loft. Once the apartment had a clean bill of health, they said, they'd be getting two more birds. As I was reading the e-mail, Rhett and Scarlett came through again and asked me to tell their dads that once they got the birds, they would reincarnate and go into their bodies. Needless to say, John and David were absolutely thrilled to know they'd have them back again.

Mamie and Ike Make a Comeback

Gina's two cats, Mamie and Ike, were littermates who lived to be twenty-one years old and passed over within days of one another. They were indoor cats who had been pampered and spoiled, and they lived a wonderful life. Neither of them had any real health issues until about a year before they died, when they were very old and had developed arthritis.

Ike went first, in his sleep, and Mamie was devastated. Even though she could still sense him around her, she missed his physical body so much that she didn't want to keep going without him. When Gina booked a reading with me, Mamie let me know that she wanted to be with Ike. She knew that she was old, too, and she was ready to go. Sure enough, she stopped eating and passed over just three days later.

After that, Gina booked another reading. This time her mother, who had died when Gina was only twelve years old, came through with Mamie and Ike in her arms. She was telling Gina that they were very happy to be together again and that they would both be back with her in her lifetime. Gina asked me if this were actually possible, which, of course, I assured her it was.

Then her mother told me that Gina was wearing a ruby ring that had belonged to her. Quietly Gina said that the ring was the only thing she had of her mother's and that she never took it off.

Well, I said, *your mother's got a couple of black cats with her as well.* And Gina said they'd been the first cats she'd ever had. She said she'd grown up with them and when her mother died they had mourned a lot, too.

She wanted to know if I could tell her when Mamie and Ike would be coming back, and I had to tell her that I didn't know. *Some animals come back very quickly, and others take a long time,* I said, *but I do know that they will be back with you in this lifetime.*

Gina was okay with that, and, in fact, it wasn't until ten years later that they both returned. By that time she had a five-year-old Boston terrier named Maisie. Her sister often came to visit with her own cat, Jack, and on one visit she suggested that they go to the shelter and get two cats for Gina. Gina wasn't sure at first, because she already had Maisie, but in the end they did go, and by the time they got to the shelter she was feeling really good about what she was about to do. Looking at so many homeless animals made her feel very sad and she decided to take two kittens who were snuggled up together in one cage, but when she told the attendant she wanted to take them both, the attendant informed her that the female had already been spoken for.

Gina was quite upset because she thought it would be very wrong to separate them. The attendant then told her that the people who were adopting the female were still at the shelter because they wanted to adopt a puppy at the same time so that the two could grow up together. She described the family to Gina, who went looking for them. When she found them, she approached and told them that she would like to take both of the kittens because they would be devastated to be separated, and the people had no problem with that. In fact, they said they'd also been drawn to another of the kittens and would be quite happy to take that one.

As Gina told me, she knew it was meant to be, because if she'd gotten to the shelter even an hour later the female kitten would have been gone and she would never even have known it. She took the two of them home and got out Mamie's and Ike's beds, which, she said, she hadn't been able to part with in all the years since they'd been gone. One was pink and the other blue, and, amazingly, as soon as the kittens saw them, the little girl went straight to the pink bed and the boy went to the blue one.

Then, when she put out food and water for them, the little female put her paw in the water and started to splash it all over the place, exactly the way Mamie had done. Gina was astonished. *Sonya,* she said, *I knew then that after all that time I had really gotten them back. For the first time since Mamie and Ike died, the pain of losing them finally went away.*

Happily, they also bonded with Maisie, and the three of them now often sleep all squashed together in Maisie's bed.

THREE

Does My Pet Know
How Much I Loved Him?

Martin told me that he thought of himself as a pretty tough guy, certainly not one to get all "gooey and goofy," as he put it, over an animal. So when he contacted me after losing his Persian cat, whom he called Poobah, he was almost apologetic. *You know, Sonya*, he said, *this is pretty embarrassing for me. I wouldn't say this to any of my friends because they'd think I was nuts, but I really need to know whether Poobah understood how much I loved her. I'm not the kind of guy who wears his heart on his sleeve, and maybe I didn't always tell her how important she was to me. I didn't always take the time to pet her and talk to her, but I loved her a lot. I miss her more than I ever imagined I would, and I just need to know that she knows that.*

We're all different in the ways we express our emotions,

and while some of us are constantly telling our animals how much we love them, others may feel a bit embarrassed about verbalizing their feelings. We humans sometimes find it difficult to say those words to one another, much less to a pet. And even when people do tell their pets how much they love them, they may not be convinced that the animal really understands.

I could hear the shakiness in Martin's voice over the phone, and I knew that he was really trying to hold himself together. He seemed to think there was something odd about what he was saying, and he didn't want to sound weak or foolish. But, as I told him immediately, absolutely everyone who loses a pet wants to know if the animal understood how much he was loved.

As Poobah communicated to me telepathically, she was sad to hear that Martin could doubt that she knew how much he loved her. He didn't need to say it out loud for her to know that, and he certainly had no reason to feel guilty. In fact, she was hoping that *he* understood how much *she* loved *him*. And she wanted him to know that, because of her love, she would always remain connected to him.

As I delivered her message to Martin, he finally let go and wept, both for the loss of his pet and for the joy of knowing that their love for one another had been mutually felt and appreciated.

Of course, I would hope that we all tell our pets how much we love them all the time, but, as I explained to Martin, when we love an animal companion, we are constantly emanating the energy of that love, like radio waves, into the electromagnetic field of the universe, and our animals feel it, not only while they are with us physically but also in the world of spirit, because, on the soul level, there is no separation between one plane and the other.

You may have had the experience of walking into a group of people and feeling that the energy in the room was either positive or negative. We all send out energy all the time, and when that energy is positive and loving, it attracts loving energy in return. Animals feel our loving energy when they're in their physical bodies, and they continue to feel it in the spirit world. We don't stop loving a pet who has crossed over to that higher plane, and our pets continue to feel our vibrational, loving energy after they have passed.

The Man Who Rescued Donkeys

George is a wonderful, spiritual animal lover who, as a young man, had spent two years traveling the world with a backpack and learning about the beliefs of many different cultures. After retiring from the technology business he'd owned, he moved to a ranch where he could rescue and take care of animals. He'd found his two donkeys, Sweetpea and Willow, doing hard labor in the fields for a farmer in Spain, where he was visiting his sister. George bought the donkeys from the farmer, and his sister agreed to look after them until he could arrange for them to be flown to the States. When he got them, their feet were so sore that they could hardly walk and they also had serious back problems from carrying such heavy loads.

Over time, George grew very close to the donkeys, and it gave him great joy to watch them recover and be well again.

I could tell as soon as I began to communicate with the donkeys how much Sweetpea and Willow loved each other, and I knew that they'd been together in past lives.

When I communicate with animals who have been abused, I can feel the pain in my own body where they are in pain, and they can communicate what's happened to them in their lives so that their rescuer and the veterinarian are better able to understand how to help them. Although Sweetpea and Willow would always remain in delicate health, with George they were able to live out their lives in love, joy, and peace. Love is the greatest healer, and George did everything in his power to ensure their physical comfort, including building a barn for them that was air-conditioned and heated and that they could go in and out of at will. There were even times when they first arrived and weren't feeling well that George would sleep in the barn with them. With him, they were living in the donkey equivalent of a Four Seasons hotel.

The three of them truly loved one another, and the donkeys followed George everywhere. Each morning when he got up, he went out to the barn with his coffee and two apples. The coffee was for him and the apples were for the donkeys.

They'd both been up in years when he got them, and eventually the time came to help Sweetpea move on. George called me then and said that before he put Sweetpea to sleep he wanted to talk to her. I asked her if she was ready to leave her body, and she said that she was hurting but she didn't want to go without Willow.

George knew how much they loved each other, especially with all they'd been through together, and he didn't want Sweetpea to suffer anymore, but he also wasn't quite ready for Willow to leave. It was a difficult situation. George knew that Willow would be heartbroken to lose Sweetpea's physical body, but he also knew that there was really no separation, and he asked Sweetpea if she'd be willing to leave Willow with him for a little while longer. After thinking about it for a moment, she said, *Just for a little while longer.* She then went on to say how happy he'd made both their lives and that they never could have imagined they could be so happy. *I know he's heartbroken,* she said to me, *but you know and I know that we'll never leave him.*

Willow then said that he'd stay a bit longer with George, but that he'd be joining Sweetpea very soon. A week later George phoned to say that after Sweetpea went, Willow had stopped eating, and that he, too, had passed a few days later. *You were right,* he said. *He only stayed for a little while. Please tell them I'm so happy that they're together again.*

He also told me that he still took his coffee and their apples out to the barn every day, at which point Sweetpea chimed in from the spiritual world and said, *That's right, and he also eats the apples!* For the first time, George laughed, and he said, *I do. And tell them I'm going to do it for the rest of my life because I know they're with me. And please tell them that when I get up every morning my first thought is of them.*

He told me that after they were gone he could feel them around him, and I said, *Oh, George, I wish you could see what I see. I see them running together into a sunset, and I can feel all their joy.*

Sonya, he replied. *I know you're right.* And then he burst out laughing and said, *I know they're there, and I can feel happy for them. We both know better than to be getting into all this physical sadness!*

Henry and Sandypuss Love Theo

Theo had two beautiful Ragdoll cats, Henry and Sandypuss. Sandypuss was the first to go, and Henry lived to be nineteen. But when Theo booked a reading, Henry told me that he was also ready to go. He had kidney problems, liver problems, and very severe arthritis that kept him in so much pain that there were times when he just didn't want to move at all, even to use his litter box. He asked me to please let Theo know that he'd had a wonderful time living with him and his best friend, Sandypuss, but he was now ready to move on and return to his home in the spiritual realm.

Theo knew it was Henry's time and was devastated at the thought of having to go on without him. But he was also very aware of Henry's pain, so he told me to please let his beloved animal know that he would help him go over and to explain that the vet would be coming to the house the next day to euthanize him. Then he asked if he should put the phone next to Henry's ear so that he could hear me. Many people ask me this, but, as I explained to Theo, telepathic language travels through magnetic fields, not through telephone lines. All animals communicate telepathically with one another as well as with humans, and they understand how the silent language works.

As we were talking, Theo broke down in tears, but Henry had some heartwarming news for him. He said that he would reincarnate very soon because, as he put it, *No other cat is going to take over my home and my wonderful dad. So please tell Theo that he needs to get another cat, because I can't come back until he does, and it would be very nice if he got two, because then Sandypuss could come back, too.*

When I delivered that message, Theo thanked me and said that knowing Henry understood how much he was loved and wanted to come back made it a bit easier to let him go.

Three months later, when he booked another appointment

with me, Theo said that he'd been to the pound and seen a three-year-old cat with whom he'd felt an immediate bond. *Sonya*, he said, *there was a connection there. I'd seen several other cats, but as soon as I approached the cage this one was in, he came right up and reached his paw out to me. I had such an immediate feeling of love that I just knew he was the one for me. The amazing thing was that as soon as I brought him home, he ran right into my bedroom, as if he knew exactly where it was, jumped up on the bed, and went right to sleep in the same spot on the pillow that Henry had always slept in. But,* he said, *I don't feel that this is either Henry or Sandypuss. He did seem to know things Henry would have known, but he's also different in many ways.*

Well, you know, Theo, I told him, *when an animal returns from the spiritual realm it won't be exactly the same as it was in its previous life. Your new cat will have his own personality, but you will start to see bits of Henry in him. Also, it can sometimes take a while for animals to enter a new physical body. They may go in and out, over and over again, before they settle in permanently.*

Theo said he would be patient, and I didn't hear from him for quite a while after that. But then he booked another reading. This time he immediately said, *Sonya, they've come back to me!*

Oh, I said, *so you've got two cats now.*

No, Theo replied, *I've got three! What happened was this. I'd gone to do some grocery shopping at Walmart, and as I was putting the bags in the trunk of my car I felt something rubbing against* my leg. I looked down and there was a little kitten. I picked it up, and as I was holding it, a woman came up to me holding another kitten she said she'd just found under her car. She said she'd take both of them to the pound, but I knew that if she did that they'd both be put down, so I told her to give the one she had to me. She handed it over and as soon as I had both of them in my arms I felt totally peaceful and happy. The woman looked at me and smiled. "It was meant to be for you, then," she said. And I knew she was right. I knew they had found me and not the other way around. One is the spitting image of Sandypuss, and I know now I've got them both back. When I spoke to you the last time I wasn't so sure, but as time went on I began to see more and more of Henry's traits in my new cat. And the third one is simply a joy—an added bonus.

I never imagined I'd have three, but now I have so much fun in my life. Every time a walk through the door they all run to greet me, and I'm just so happy. When Henry went I didn't think I'd ever be happy again, but now my life has completely turned around.

The Cat Who Crossed the Road

When Mary Beth got on the phone with me, she was distraught. She had two cats in the spirit world and simply couldn't get over their loss. Some of us have an easier time than others navigating through life, and, unfortunately, Mary Beth was one of those who made things even more difficult for herself than they needed to be. In her mind, the only unconditional love she'd ever received in her life was that she got from her cats.

One of the first things she said to me was that one day her cat Tiger had simply disappeared and she absolutely "knew" her former boyfriend had in some way been responsible for his death. When I tuned in to Tiger, I could feel that he'd died very young—at about the age of four—and Mary Beth confirmed that this was true. Then she said, *Ask him what my ex-boyfriend did to him.*

Absolutely nothing, I told her. Then Tiger began to relate his story to me. He told me that he was an indoor/outdoor cat and that he'd gone out one morning and run fast across the road as he always did. On this morning, however, he was hit by a car going at full speed and it "bowled him over." He'd kept running, but then he dropped to the ground and died. I could also feel that Tiger didn't hear very well (which, again, Mary Beth confirmed) and that he hadn't heard the car coming. He said that he'd jumped out of his body and when he looked down he couldn't believe it, because he could see his physical body lying in the road. As I explained to Mary Beth, this sometimes happens when we leave our body and go into spirit.

Then, he said, he saw a cat he'd known before who'd also passed over. He said the other cat often came to his yard and walked along the fence. And he also saw a dog who used to walk past his house with his human companion. *All I could feel was love,* he told me, and I could feel that love coming from him. He also said that he was very happy, that he could move freely, and that he felt very light in his energy body. Mary Beth was an emotional wreck, but Tiger said that he had come straight back to her, as our animals often do, because there is really no separation. *Tell her I'm sitting on the back of her chair right now,* he said. And when I told this to Mary Beth, she gasped and said, *Oh, Sonya, that's exactly where he always sat.*

At that point Whiskers, her other cat in spirit, also came through. Whiskers seemed to be a lot older, and Mary Beth said that he'd lived to be sixteen. He also told me that he'd moved with her many times, and that they had both gone to live with her mother. *I was really happy to be settled down,* he said, *and not to be moving around anymore.* Although Mary Beth was thrilled that Whiskers had come through as well, she was less than kind in her assessment of her relationship with her mother. As much as she was able to show her love for her cats, she was simply a person who couldn't seem to get along with other people.

They're still around you, you know, I told her, and she said that she did feel that and she talked to them all the time. *Well, that's good,* I said. *They're telling me that you're still living in your mother's house.*

Yes, Mary Beth said. *She left it to me after I'd nursed her through her last illness, but it's the only good thing she ever did for me in my life.*

At that point, Whiskers started talking to me again. He

told me that after he'd first been diagnosed with cancer he had recovered and been well for quite a long period of time. *That's right*, Mary Beth said. *The vet told me that he wouldn't live for more than a month. So I took him home and one night while he was with me on the bed I told him that I wouldn't want to go on living without him. I know he understood me. And then I felt something very peculiar.*

I know what you felt, I said. *You felt a shift in your energy.*

Yes, I felt something shift, she said. *And that night Tiger was in my dreams. I could see him in a beautiful white light, and he came up to me and touched me with his paw, and he told me that Whiskers wasn't going to die. I'd never felt so happy in my entire life. And when I woke up in the morning, I felt so much better. Then, a few days later, I was on the bed again with Whiskers and again I felt something shift, and from that day on Whiskers started to get better. After a couple of weeks he was his old self again, and when I took him to the vet he couldn't figure out what had happened.*

I can tell you what happened, I said. *When Tiger left his physical body, he was young and his body was very healthy. What you felt was Tiger's energy going into Whiskers' body and healing it. Tiger and Whiskers had actually been together in a past life, and even before they went into their physical bodies they knew this was going to happen. It's part of your karma, and it's a great gift you've been given.*

The cats are telling me that you need to learn from this. You need to stop worrying and making up stories about other people that aren't really true, because all you're doing is making your own life more stressful than it needs to be. Your cats are helping you to heal just the way that Tiger healed Whiskers. Miracles do happen!

Thank you so much for explaining all that, Mary Beth said. *I could never figure out what had happened, but it all makes sense to me now.*

You and your cats are very close, I said, and, of course, she agreed. *You've shared many past lives,* I told her, *and you deserve to have this miracle in this lifetime. Life isn't an easy journey, but everything helps us to learn. So, please, learn from this experience, because your cats have taught you so much in death as well as in life. No one on this earth plane has an easy journey, but we can make it easier by looking at things in a loving way. They've taught you how to love, so for the rest of your life they want you to look at life like this.*

Mary Beth wanted to know if Tiger and Whiskers would be coming back, and they told me they wouldn't. *She needs to learn this lesson on her own,* they said. Then she asked me if she should get another cat, and I told her she absolutely should. *The shelters are full of cats who need rescuing,* I said. *Why not get two more? You seem to have so much love and happiness with your animals.*

Mary Beth then told me that she'd been feeling guilty because she thought Tiger and Whiskers wouldn't want her to do that. So I had to remind her again that in the spirit world there is nothing but love, and that her cats wanted her to experience that love and happiness again. *Tiger and Whiskers are incredible souls,* I said. *You've already learned so much from them. They gave you love; they taught you how to love; and from the spirit world they're sending you wisdom. That's what it's all about, so, please, listen to what they're telling you.*

FOUR

Was My Pet Happy with Me?
Did I Take Good Care of Him?

Most of us do whatever we can to take good care of our animals, but we all do things we regret. We all have circumstances in our lives that are beyond our control. And because we can never be sure that our well-loved animals understand how hard we try to care for them or why we sometimes need to do something that might make them unhappy, the guilt can eat away at our hearts, especially after they are gone, and make our grief even more difficult to bear.

You know, Sonya, I sometimes had to leave Oscar with my mom when I traveled on business, and I always worried that he wasn't happy with her or that he thought I was abandoning him. Since I got him as a rescue dog, I'm sure he'd had a difficult life before he came to me, and I just really need to know that he was happy with me and that I took good care of him. I don't want to be like one of those parents whose children grow up angry with them and who then just say, "Well, I did the best I could." But that's sometimes how I feel, and I really need to know that my best was good enough for Oscar.

Even though I couldn't see Martha's expression as we talked on the phone, I could hear the guilt and deep regret in her voice. I knew that Martha was distraught, but I also knew that she truly had nothing to regret and no reason to be beating herself up, at least so far as Oscar was concerned.

Oscar was a big, hairy mixed breed, and when he came through to me I could see from the expression in his soft brown eyes that she didn't need to have those terrible self-doubts. He was able to let me know that he had, indeed, had some troubles before Martha adopted him, but he had known from the minute she took him home that he was in a safe place and had finally found a loving human companion. In fact, his earlier experiences had made him even more appreciative not only of how much she loved him, but also of how well she took care of him. Of course, he missed her when she had to go away, but he told me that her mother had also loved him and had always been kind to him, and he had loved her, too, if not in the same way he loved Martha. If Oscar was unhappy at all now, it was because he was worried about Martha, knowing how much she still worried about him!

I explained to Martha that when we're happy, our animal companions are happy, too. When we're tense or sad or stressed, they feel those vibrations, the same way they feel our love, and they absorb and reflect our emotions. Martha was much relieved to know that she hadn't "disappointed" Oscar and that he was not only happy but also deeply appreciative of the loving-kindness she had always shown him. He also wanted to let her know that he was still with her and that they never needed to be separated again.

By the end of our conversation Martha was in tears, but, as she told me, they were tears of relief to know that she hadn't fallen short, and that Oscar had always known that.

Mr. Turtle

I met Erin at an event the great psychic John Edward was doing in Houston, and she booked an appointment for me to do a reading with her beautiful white turtle, who was simply known as Mr. Turtle. I've spoken with many turtles in my day, but never before a white one. White turtles are quite rare, and this one was also extremely intelligent. As soon as I picked up the phone, Mr. Turtle came through and started talking a mile a minute. Erin had explained to him that he'd be speaking to someone who spoke his language, and he immediately asked me if I was a turtle. I said that at that moment I was a turtle but I was also a human. *How can that be?* he asked. *Well,* I said, *many things can be. I was born with a hearing loss and when I was a little girl the animals all taught me their languages.* And he accepted that.

The first thing he told me was how much he loved the water in the pond where he lived. Erin laughed and said that she and her husband had gotten Mr. Turtle in Florida and the water there was terrible. So they'd made him a special pond inside the house with filtered water, and they kept it very clean. Erin said she was happy that he appreciated what they'd done, because they really wanted him to be happy, and I was able to assure her that, indeed, he was deliriously happy.

Mr. Turtle went on to tell me that he loved the beautiful, huge rocks in the pond and also the fish they'd put in it even though they didn't seem to swim very well. Erin laughed again and told me that they were toy fish, but Mr. Turtle said he loved the fish and wanted me to thank her. He also wanted her to know that he loved it when people came and sat by the pond talking to him. He was very proud that people wanted to visit with him.

As he was telling me all this, I had the feeling that Mr. Turtle hadn't been feeling very well, and Erin confirmed that. *But,* he said, *she gave me some antibiotics. Do you know what those are?* So I explained that antibiotics were medicine to make him well, and Mr. Turtle asked me to thank her because he was feeling much better now.

At that point I could see another white turtle coming toward me in the spirit world, and Erin said they'd had one who'd died a few weeks before. I could feel that he'd had worms in his stomach, and even though Erin said they'd given him antibiotics, it was too late and they couldn't save him. That's one of the reasons why they were now being so careful with Mr. Turtle.

Then I saw a gentleman coming through in spirit who told me that he'd taught Erin how to ride a bicycle, that he was always around her, and that he also liked her husband. *Oh,* said Erin, *that's my uncle. He spent a lot of time with me when I was growing up. Please tell him I love him and he can come visit me whenever he wants.*

Her uncle then told me that he was with the turtle in spirit and that neither one of them was coming back because they were both so happy over there. He also said that Erin had an aunt, his sister, who had dementia, who was very frightened of going over. *Yes,* Erin said. *She's ninety-eight and she should go.* So her uncle said that he was going to tell his sister it was about time and that he would take her over. *It won't be long,* he said.

Mr. Turtle then started to talk again, telling me that a little boy had come to visit and that he didn't like him very much because the boy had been splashing his feet in the turtle's pond and he definitely didn't appreciate that. *Tell Erin not to let that kid come again,* he said. Erin told me it was her nephew and that she'd make sure he didn't do that again.

After that Mr. Turtle said that he hoped to live a long time, and I told him I hoped so, too.

Erin asked if there was anything else he would like, and I told her that he seemed to be very happy just as he was. But he did ask me if they were getting a cat, and Erin said they'd considered it but had decided not to in case the cat somehow hurt Mr. Turtle. *Well,* he said, *thank goodness for that. We don't want any cats in this house! I'm enjoying getting all the attention myself.*

The only thing he wasn't so happy about was that they'd changed his food, and Erin said that the vet had recommended it. *Well,* said Mr. Turtle, *the vet doesn't know. Tell her to change it back.* So Erin said she'd talk to the vet about it. *Ha,* said the turtle. *I'd like to hear what the vet would say if she told him she'd been talking to me!*

Then he thanked me for talking with him and said that he hoped we'd be able to talk again in the future. I told him I hoped so, too.

In fact, that was one of the most entertaining communications I'd ever had with any animal in either the physical or the spiritual world. I think it shows that all animals do know when they are loved and appreciate whatever we do to make their lives as happy and healthy as possible.

For the Love of Alice

Alice, a Boston terrier mix, was the beloved pet of Sylvia and Nancy, who had rescued her from the pound when she was about a year old. Sylvia had always believed that she was very

special, and that she had the ability to heal. Sylvia was a breast cancer survivor and said that Alice had been with her every moment throughout her ordeal, lying on the bed right next to her. I know that animals' love is extremely powerful, and in Sylvia's mind Alice really had played a role in her healing process.

Both Sylvia and Nancy adored her, but she appeared to have a special bond with Sylvia, who told me that if she was in the kitchen, Alice would follow her; if she went to the bathroom, Alice was there. *The love she gave to me was overwhelming,* Sylvia said on the telephone. *It filled the house; we could feel it everywhere.*

Tragically, a few months after Sylvia's recovery, when Alice was only five years old, she, too, was diagnosed with cancer. The vet told Sylvia and Nancy that she had a large tumor in her abdomen and that they should put her to sleep because the tumor could burst, and if it did she would have a very painful death. Both Nancy and Sylvia were devastated, but, as they told me, they had explained to Alice what was happening and that they were going to ask the vet to come to the house to help her return to the world of spirit. They told her it was okay for her to go back home, and she went out of her body very peacefully. As they were telling me all this, Sylvia broke down.

Oh, Sonya, she cried, *I think I gave her cancer because she spent so much time with me while I was recovering. Did I give her cancer?* she sobbed, *because if I did, please ask her to forgive me.*

Of course, I assured her that she hadn't given Alice cancer, which is not a contagious disease. I explained that Alice's time had simply come, and that it was a pity it had come so soon. *But,* I said, *I can see her in the spirit world. She's with a little black dog and they're running and jumping in a beautiful green meadow, just having a great old time.*

Oh, Sylvia said, *that's Rupert. They were best friends, and they used to run around the yard like two mad dogs, jumping over one another.*

Well, I told her, *Alice is telling me that Rupert was waiting to take her over, and now they're together again. You know, we never have to apologize to our pets for anything. I know you didn't give Alice cancer, but however you think you may have been guilty of something during her lifetime, she would never judge you. Animals don't judge. They simply love. And Alice is letting me know that you and Nancy were the kindest, most loving and compassionate human companions she could ever have had.*

At that point, I could also see a beautiful woman coming toward me with a German shepherd dog at her side. When I described her, Sylvia immediately said, *Oh, that's my mother, and that's the dog we had when I was growing up.*

Well, Sylvia, I said, *your mother is telling me that when you and Nancy have finished your work on the earth plane, they're all going to be waiting for you on the other side, but she's also asking me to remind you that they don't expect you just yet! "We all love you and we'll be watching over you from here" they say.* You know, I told both women, *there really is no separation. You may feel the*

separation now, but as you learn to live without Alice's physical body, you'll begin to feel her around you.

They wanted to know if Alice would be coming back to them, and I said, *Not in this lifetime, but, you know, a lifetime is really a very short while, and you'll meet with her again when you go over.*

A couple of weeks later, I received an e-mail from them saying that, the night before, they had heard Alice's nails clicking on the floor, and they could feel the mattress sink when she jumped up on the bed. *She was letting us know that she hadn't gone anywhere, and we were absolutely overwhelmed with joy.*

It's often amazing to me what people feel guilty about and think they need to apologize for when they lose an animal. But, as I continue to say, animals love their humans no matter what, and there's never any need to apologize.

A Boy Grieves for His Pet

Liz had booked an appointment with me because her fourteen-year-old son, Ryan, couldn't get over the death of his cat, Remi. I could tell that Ryan was a very loving soul, and this had been his first big loss. As soon as we got on the phone I saw a big black cat in spirit. I generally take calls from my private clients while sitting on my bed, and as the black cat came forward it jumped right onto the bed beside me and walked around as if he owned it. I could tell that he was a very confident cat. There was also another, very sweet cat named Max coming through, who I knew was still in his physical body. Ryan had always considered Remi his cat while Max belonged to Liz, even though they each loved both of the family cats.

Liz had told me that she and her son listened to my radio program every week, so I knew that he understood how I work. As I started to talk to them, the black cat in spirit told me that he had died very quickly. I could hear the noise of a car engine and feel the impact in my body, so I knew that he had been hit by the car. Liz and Ryan confirmed that this was true, and they were extremely excited that I had made contact with him.

Children love their animals very much and will often tell them things that they can't or won't tell their parents, and Remi had been Ryan's closest confidant. *You talked to him all the time, didn't you?* I said to him, *because he never judged you; he just loved you unconditionally.*

That's right, he said. *I told him everything.*

Then Remi started to tell me about his wonderful life with Ryan and Liz. Remi's favorite game was when Ryan was in bed and moved his feet under the covers. Remi would pretend that the feet were monsters and that he was attacking them. He also said that if Ryan stopped doing it, Remi would start walking around his head, which really annoyed him, until he started to move his feet again. Ryan laughed and said that was absolutely correct and that he used to get annoyed when Remi kept walking around his head. *But now,* he said, *it's one of the things I miss most.*

Ryan and Remi really had a great understanding between them, and although Ryan wasn't yet consciously aware of it, he was already beginning to understand his animal's language. Many people actually have this ability, even though they don't recognize it in themselves. *You know,* I said to Ryan, *you've been a cat in past lives and so has your mom. That's why you both have such a great understanding of them.*

Wow, Ryan said, *my mother and I have always said that to one another, and I've always known how cats feel and what they sense.*

At that point, Max also started talking to me. He wasn't about to be left out of the conversation. He was telling me that he and Remi had been best friends and he missed his friend a lot, but he also said that they were very different. Max was very easygoing while Remi was very curious, very determined, and a big show-off. Whenever they had visitors, Max said, Remi would march right out to be admired while Max didn't show himself until he'd decided whether or not he liked the visitors. And, according to Max, he was also much better looking than Remi. I told him that they were both beautiful in their own ways, and I also thanked him for telling me so much about Remi but said that I'd like to talk to him directly if that was okay.

Max told me that would be fine, and he also said that he'd

sensed, a few days before Remi died, that he would be passing quite soon. Animals are very psychic, and they do sometimes have these kinds of premonitions. I could tell that he was also grieving and that he missed his playmate.

At that point Ryan spoke up, and I knew he was feeling much better just knowing that both Remi and Max were communicating with me. In fact, Remi then came through again and told me that Ryan wasn't very good at math but he loved to play baseball and that he was very good at it. He also said that since he was now in the spirit world he could go with Ryan to all his baseball games. *Ryan,* I said, *Remi is always with you. He goes to school with you and he goes with you when you play baseball. In fact, he's telling me that you don't like math very much and that when you grow up you're going to be a baseball player.*

That's exactly right, Ryan said. *I don't like math and I'm not very good at it, and I always used to tell him that I wanted to be a famous baseball player one day.*

Well, he knows that, I told him. *He knows everything about you.*

But, he said, *I'm really finding it painful living without him.*

I know, Ryan, I said. *That's the worst part. Whenever we lose an animal, no matter how many we lose, we always feel the same pain. The first time it happens, it's the most painful experience you've ever encountered. But you'll always have animals in your life, and it's all part of having animals.*

Remi is out of his body and he's out of pain and now he can go everywhere with you. He's telling me that he was even with you when you found his body on the road. He was already out of his body then and walking right behind you. I know you're going to keep remembering how terrible it was to find his body, but when you do that you have to understand that the body is just an old car we travel in. He climbed out of that body just like we climb out of a car. Whenever you relive that experience, just remind yourself that it was a very nice car he traveled in, but he had to get out of it because it hit a big bump. Thinking of it like that will help you to deal with the memories.

Thank you, Sonya, Ryan said. *I hadn't thought of it that way. That really helps me.*

You know, Ryan, I told him, *you're really fortunate to have the kind of knowing you do. You'll feel Remi with you, and he'll always be with both you and your mother. Your mother is a very special lady, and she's taught you wisdom. She arranged this reading with me because she knew how much it would help you. We don't get over these things; we just learn to live with them.*

Well, I know now that my cat's always with me, he said. *Will he come to school with me?*

Well, I said, *he's already said that he will. And wherever you go, when you think about him he'll be right there at your side.*

As I hung up the phone, I couldn't help thinking how lucky Ryan was to have such an enlightened mother, because so many children don't know where their animals go or where they are, and they grieve for a very long time. Some children never get over the death of their first animal.

FIVE

Is My Animal Still with Me?
Will He Come Back?

For most of us these days, our pets are part of the family. They're our constant companions, our loyal friends, and they seem to sense and empathize with our moods even when no one else does. For many they're as close as children; for some they may be our only children. And while most of us can expect that our children will outlive us, sadly, our pets almost never do. It's hard for most people to believe that their animal companions remain a loving presence in their lives after they've left the earth plane, but they do. And sometimes, as we've already discussed, they actually reincarnate—as do people—by going into the body of another living creature, although some also choose to remain in the spiritual realm. Whether or not they come back, however, they will remain connected to us. I've seen the truth of that demonstrated over and over, and I've never spoken to anyone whose animal didn't connect and come through to me immediately to reassure them of that presence.

I still love my pussycat Penny so much that I don't know how I'm going to live without her, and I just have to know if she still loves me, too. I know she loved me when we were together, but now that she isn't sitting on my lap and purring or licking my hand, I just don't know if she still loves me the way I love her. I don't even know why it matters so much, but you say that our animals stay connected to us even after they cross into the spirit world, and I guess I think that the only reason for her to keep that connection, which means so much to me, would be if she still loved me as much as I continue to love her.

Stephanie sounded almost hysterical as she spilled out her fears over the phone, but I was able to put her mind at rest. *Stephanie,* I said, *you sound so sad, but you really must stop worrying. Penny's sitting on the back of the sofa right now. She's right up by your shoulder and she wants to know why humans don't understand that their pets love them unconditionally and never stop loving them even in the spirit world. And by the way, she said to tell you that she still sleeps on the pillow right next to your head every night.*

At that point I could feel that Stephanie was smiling through her tears. *Oh, Sonya,* she said, laughing, *that's exactly where she always slept, with her little head right next to mine!* Since no one but Stephanie could have known that, she was instantly reassured of Penny's continued presence. It was clear not only that Penny still loved her, but also that she continued to be with Stephanie and watch over her from the world of spirit.

Doing the Right Thing

Sandra loved her Labrador, Jake, more than anyone in her life; she got him when he was just six weeks old and they'd been inseparable ever since. He was a great traveler who went everywhere with her and loved riding in the car. The only time she hadn't been with him, she told me, was when she had emergency surgery for appendicitis and left him with her mother until she was able to take care of him again.

When Jake's time came to leave and return to the spirit world Sandra was devastated, and she said over and over, *I want to die to be with him. When he goes, I want to go, too.*

Jake was very ill with stomach cancer, but our dogs will hang on because they love us so much and they are very good at tolerating discomfort and pain. Jake was sixteen, a good age for a Lab, but Sandra just couldn't let him go. Between sobs she said, *I can't put him down. I know he's suffering, but I just can't do it.* Jake's body was worn out. He couldn't walk—his back legs gave out on him—and his arthritis was painful. He was also going blind, and much to his own disgust he could no longer control his bladder. This caused him great distress, as he told me that he had always been a very clean dog. He was a very dignified dog. I could feel his painful body, and more so his distress.

I said to Sandra, *Imagine yourself in his situation. How would you feel if you were incontinent and you couldn't walk and you were in great pain? I don't think there's anywhere in his body that is not in pain.*

At the same time, he wasn't eating, and I told Sandra that he was going to starve to death. I don't often say this to people, but I said, *Please, put him to sleep. He has no quality of life and he's really suffering. Do you want him to starve to death?* And then, unbelievably, she said she was going to ask the vet to force-feed him. I told her I didn't think the vet would agree to that. I explained that she really had to let Jake go and that she was actually being very selfish and, although I was sure she didn't intend it, cruel. *Put him to sleep,* I said. *You owe it to him to help him into the spirit world where he will no longer be in pain.*

I know that letting go of our animals is a very hard thing to do, but I find that most people don't want their animals to suffer. They have great compassion, and they know that the animal is just hanging on for his human companion. They do that; no matter how much they're suffering, they hang on. I said to Sandra, *You must tell him it's okay to go. Now that you know how he feels and how much he's suffering, how do you feel?*

And of course she started to cry. She said, *Then I'm going to go with him, I'm going to commit suicide.* So I said, *Oh, Sandra, if you do that you'll have to come right back here and go through a whole other life starting as a baby, and you won't be with him anyway. It's wrong to commit suicide, because that means you're ending your life before your work here is done. That means you have to come back and relive those years. You might have had five years or twenty years left, but however long it was, you're going to have to finish out the life you cut short. If you help Jake go over, he'll come right back to you in spirit, but if you take your own life, you'll just be prolonging your separation.*

Finally she agreed that she would try to do it. I said again, *I know how hard it is, but, Sandra, there's a young man coming through to me now holding a crash helmet.* Then she started crying again, and she said, *That's my brother, Harry. He died in a motorcycle accident when he was eighteen.*

Her brother started to tell me that he wanted Sandra to know he loved her, and she said she loved him, too. For the first time I heard joy in her voice. Then he started to talk about the dog they'd had when they were growing up, and I saw a dog with him in the spirit world. It was a beagle. I told Sandra that Harry was playing with a beagle, and that he said to tell her to let Jake come over. He said he'd be waiting for him and would take care of him. He also told me that Sandra wore her watch on her right wrist. And she said, *Oh, he's talking about the watch of his I've had since he died. I know that's him.* So I said, *Sandra, you know he's alive in spirit and Jake will be, too. There's no separation. Only the physical body dies. We travel back home. There's life on this earth plane but there's also life on the other side. You know that because your brother is coming through for you.* And again Harry said, *Let him come over, let go of him. I'll be with you, and as he comes out of his body I'll be here for him.*

At that point Sandra did a total turnaround. She started to laugh. She said, *You were always there for me, weren't you?* And he said, *Let him go and we'll come and see you constantly.* Finally Sandra asked me to tell Harry how much she loved him and that she was going to let Jake go.

I felt tremendous relief coming from Jake, because even though he wanted to hang on he knew that his body wouldn't let him and he'd have to go very soon. I told Sandra to just tell Jake it was okay to go, because that would help him to feel easier about passing, and, I said, *Don't worry. He won't be leaving you, because there isn't any separation.*

Two months later Sandra booked another appointment to talk to Jake. I asked her how she was doing, and then I said, *Have you got another dog?* She started to laugh and said, *Yes, I have. I went to the shelter and I got another dog and I've named him Trevor.* And she sounded so happy. She sounded completely different. She said, *I'm hoping Jake will come back because I know that dogs do reincarnate.* So I told her that I'd ask Harry and Jake.

First Harry started to laugh. *I'm not going back there. I love it over here. There's nothing but peace and love and joy,* he said.

And then Jake said that he was staying with Harry in spirit and wouldn't return within Sandra's lifetime either. I told Sandra that it's a choice we all get to make in the spirit world. *Over there you can learn so much spiritually, you can go to a higher level of consciousness, and that's what Jake has chosen.*

But, her brother said, *you've got a wonderful little fellow there who was going to be put to sleep. You'll love him just as much but, in a different way.* And Sandra said to tell Harry she loved the new dog already. *For the first time,* she said, *I can accept that Jake won't come back.*

But, I said, *you'll be with him and with your brother when it's your time to go over. They'll be waiting for you.*

Since then she's been doing readings with me every few months. I talk to Trevor, and we talk to her brother and Jake in spirit. Jake tells her all the things he's been doing with her, going to restaurants and here and there. *You know,* I told her, *Jake can now go everywhere with you.* And he said, *Tell her that I'm still sleeping in the bed with her.*

Oh, Sonya, she said, *I do know that. I really do.*

The Dog Who Shook Hands

Not every story I hear from my clients involves a pet in spirit, and not every story of reincarnation is about a dog who came back. One of my favorite stories is about a very special dog named Monty, an English cocker spaniel who lived with Anita and Tom.

Anita had booked a reading with me and sent me a picture of Monty. When she called, she immediately told me that Monty was special, and as soon as I looked at the photo she had sent me I knew that he was special; I just didn't yet know how. There was a very familiar feeling coming from him, and I felt that he and Anita had been together before. *This isn't the first time this dog has been with you in this lifetime,* I said. *And he doesn't think he's a dog. He thinks he's a human, so you must treat him that way.*

Anita laughed and said, *Yes, he's the love of my life, and my husband adores him, too. We're so lucky to have him back. We know he's reincarnated.*

You've also been with him in many past lives, I went on. *And in one of those lives he was in human form. You and your husband have also been in many animal forms.*

At that point I heard her husband, Tom, laughing, and I said, *Oh, you're on the line, too.*

Absolutely, he said. *I wasn't going to miss this for anything!*

Meanwhile, Monty was telling me that Anita knew who he was before he went into his dog body. *Yes,* Anita said, laughing. *Actually the reason I called you was to find out if I was right. I knew you'd know. Monty has absolutely no behavior problems. He's the best-behaved dog you could ever find. And he has better manners than a lot of humans. He's constantly shaking hands with us.*

As she was telling me all this, Monty was letting me know that he had two homes and that he went to a lake house with Anita and Tom. *He says he has a wonderful time there and that he goes on a boat with you and jumps off to swim in the lake.* At that point Anita and Tom were both laughing out loud.

He's really telling you all that? Anita asked. *Well, yes,* I said, *and he's also saying that he reminds you of someone you loved very much who also loved to swim in the lake, and that Tom cooks him a steak all for himself every night even if no one else is eating steak.*

Yes, I do! Tom said.

It's your father, isn't it, I said to Anita. *He's come back as the dog.*

Right on! said Anita. She went on to explain that when her father was a young man he traveled all around the world and spent a lot of time in the Far East where people have a firm belief in reincarnation. At the end of his life he went to live with Tom and Anita, and a few days before he died he told her that he was going to come back to her. *I'm going to come back to you on this earth plane,* he said. *I'm going to be your dog. The next dog you get I'm coming into. We were very close,* she went on. *And Tom loved him, too. He always used to cook steaks for Tom when we went to visit him. He loved his steak, so now Tom is paying him back for what he did for us. He also built our lake house, and he swam in that lake every day, summer or winter.*

He was very psychic and told me that when he came back I

would know it. It's just so great to know that Dad is still with us. I've told this to people, and they never laugh because they've never met another dog like Monty. When friends who knew Dad come to visit, he shakes hands with them, but he never shakes hands with people Dad did not know. As soon as we got Monty as a puppy, the pain of losing my dad went away. And the reason for that, I'm sure, is that Tom, Dad, Monty, and I all knew we were back together again.

Lost and Found

Jessica, her husband, Steve, and their six-month-old baby, Peter, lived on a small ranch. While her husband worked in a nearby city, Jessica took care of the ranch chores—feeding the horses, the cattle, the free-range chickens, and the barn cats they'd inherited from the previous owners of the ranch. They also had three rescue dogs—Serge, a German shepherd dog; Sargent, a spaniel mix; and Sue, a Jack Russell terrier—whom she normally left in the house while she went about her chores with the baby strapped to her back. If she didn't do that, she said, Serge, the youngest and largest of the three, would sometimes jump the fence in the yard and chase the chickens when she let them out into the field.

On one particular morning Jessica had a very uneasy feeling in the pit of her stomach. *I just felt that something bad was going to happen, and I didn't know why,* she said to me on the phone when she called.

She said that she'd finished feeding the other animals and then went to feed the barn cats. *Normally,* she told me, *when I filled their bowls they always came running up to me to say hello, even though they didn't like me to touch them. On this morning, however, they were nowhere to be seen. I looked around and finally spotted them up in the hayloft, but they didn't come down, which had never happened before. As I was leaving, I turned around and saw that they were all eating, so I felt a bit better, although I still thought it was odd.*

Heading back up the road to the house, Jessica saw smoke pouring out of the windows and knew that the house was on fire. *I called 911 on my cell phone,* she said, *and ran as fast as I could toward the house with the baby screaming on my back. All I could think of was the dogs. I lay the baby on the lawn and opened the door. Serge was right there, so I pulled him out, but I couldn't see the other two. I called and called but they didn't come, and I couldn't get inside to look for them. There was just too much smoke and fire. At that point I could hear the fire engine coming. One of the firemen gave Serge oxygen and he started to come around, but the other two didn't make it. It was later determined that the fire had been started by some faulty electrical wiring.*

At that point I could see Sargent and Sue running toward

me in the spirit world along with a golden retriever and a young man who I felt had passed in an accident. Jessica told me that this was her brother, Dan, who had died in his twenties when his plane crashed in the mountains, and the retriever was his dog, Polly. *Jessica,* I said, *he's so happy! And all the dogs are, too. Your brother wants me to thank you for taking care of Polly after he died, and he says that he loves you very much. He's also telling me that now he has a pack because he also brought over Sargent and Sue.*

Oh, Sonya, Jessica said, *tell him I love him, too. I knew he'd come through and I knew he'd have the dogs with him. When he died it was the saddest moment of my life, and when my dogs went I felt just the same way.*

I could hear Dan laughing, and he said, *Tell my sister to get rid of that terrible picture she has of me in the den.* When I relayed the message Jessica said, *You tell him I love that picture and it's staying where it is. He'd been painting my mother's bedroom, and when he finished I just picked up the brush and painted blue streaks in his hair. My mother and I were both laughing and we took a picture of him. It brings back so many happy memories. He was my best friend.*

And he still is, I told her. Dan and the dogs had all come through to let Jessica know there was no separation when the physical body dies. *Dan is very much around you, and so are the dogs.*

Then Sargent and Sue began to tell me that they were both going to reincarnate. *But I'm not,* Dan interjected. *I'm staying here. I just feel so much peace and joy and happiness. The only way I'd return to the physical world would be as your dog. I might just do that,* he added.

While he was talking I could hear drums playing in the background, and when I mentioned that to Jessica, she said, *Oh my God, Dan used to play the drums all the time and he drove the whole family crazy with the noise.*

Well, I said, *he wants you to know that he's still playing over in the spirit world.*

Do they really do that? Jessica asked. *Well, they must,* I replied, *because he's telling me he does.*

By the time the call ended I could tell that Jessica was feeling much better. And a few months later, I heard from her again. This time, she sounded very happy. An image of two dogs, a black Lab and a Jack Russell, came into my mind. They told me that they'd always been together and that the people with whom they'd been living had driven them out into the country and left them, because they were relocating. They said that they'd run after the car for a long time until they couldn't run anymore. The Lab had been able to run farther but had gone back to find his friend. They'd been wandering around and finally arrived at Jessica's ranch. She found them near the barn eating the cats' food. They were very skinny, and she took them in and called them Angel and Goddess, because, she said, *I believe that God brought them into my life.*

She told me that Serge had accepted them at once, and since he wasn't really that easygoing she immediately wondered whether they were Sargent and Sue reincarnated. Then, she said, *I realized that they walked into the house as if they owned it. They knew where everything was, and in fact Goddess got right up on the chair Sargent had always slept in. There was no reaction at all from Serge. It was just as if my two dogs had walked back into the house. I knew then that I'd gotten them back, and the amazing thing is that, as soon as the new dogs came into my life, I no longer felt the pain of losing Sargent and Sue. I still remember the horror of what happened, but I know they've come back to me. Angel comes up and nibbles gently on my hand exactly the way Sue used to, and every time she does that I give her a big hug. I thank God every day for the wonderful miracle that happened to me.*

It's the Dog's Choice

Kelly and Mo are two great ladies and longtime clients who have become friends. They live in a charming cottage in the Hollywood hills that I helped them to decorate in a way that is both elegant and practical, because they have ten dogs living there with them. Four are Chihuahuas—Betsy, Esther, Zoe, and Daisy—and six are larger breeds named Buster, Doodle, Dan, Gertie, Henrietta, and Holly. All except one of the larger dogs had been rescued from "death row" when they were in shelters.

One day, when Kelly and Mo called me, I felt that there was something wrong with Betsy. They told me that she was missing. Their yard was fenced but somehow she'd got out. They'd been up all night calling and looking for her but hadn't been able to find her. She was micro-chipped and had contact information on her collar, but because she was so small they were really worried that she'd been run over by a car or killed by a coyote in the hills.

As I tuned in to Betsy she told me that someone had left the gate open and she'd gone out to look around. I could feel that she'd gone to the right and down a slope. She also was telling me that she'd gone past a green iron gate and that there were two dogs barking at her, one of whom had a squashed face. Then she sent me a picture of a pug. She also said that a woman had tried to get her to come but she had run away. I then felt as if I were falling and rolling over and over, so I knew she'd fallen down a steep hill. I didn't know exactly where, but I did know that she'd gone around a bend in the road before she fell. I told Kelly and Mo that she'd probably gone farther than they thought and that they should go out and look for her.

An hour later they phoned again to tell me that their Great Dane, Henrietta, had done something she'd never done before. She'd jumped the fence and taken off. She and Betsy were so closely bonded that I knew she'd gone to find her friend.

That night Kelly, Mo, and their friends all went out searching again, but they couldn't find the dogs. When they got back home, they were exhausted and fell asleep on the sofa in the den. When they woke up, they could tell that all the dogs were upset, so I spent some time talking to them and letting them know that their mothers were doing everything they could to bring their friends home.

Two days had gone by, and both Kelly and Mo were at their wit's end. They were too upset to eat but went into the kitchen to make themselves a couple of smoothies. As Kelly was looking out the kitchen window, she saw a giant Great Dane jumping over the fence with a small dog in her mouth. Henrietta had found Betsy and brought her back. When Kelly opened the door, Henrietta dropped Betsy at her feet and let out a huge joyous bark.

Betsy's leg was badly injured and she was very weak. Kelly and Mo took her to the vet immediately and Henrietta insisted on getting in the car and going with them. Betsy needed to stay at the vet and Henrietta wouldn't leave her, so Kelly and Mo let her stay. She lay down next to Betsy's crate and remained there all night. The next day they were able to take Henrietta home but, sadly, Betsy didn't make it.

After Betsy passed, Henrietta was in such deep mourning that she didn't eat for a week. So Kelly and Mo decided that they'd just have to get another little dog in the hope that it would help her. When they phoned, they told me that they'd taken Henrietta with them to the shelter. When the shelter people took out the Chihuahuas from their cages Henrietta went straight over to one, picked it up by the scruff of its neck, and dropped it at their feet as if to say, *This is the one.* They brought it home and Henrietta immediately began to recover. Kelly and Mo said they were certain that Betsy had reincarnated in the new dog's body and that's why Henrietta had chosen her.

Sonya, they said, *in a million years we never would have thought that such a miracle could happen.*

They Always Find a Way

Lavinia not only has four Dalmatians of her own, but also rescues others and finds them good homes. Molly, one of her own dogs, had recently died, and Lavinia was heartbroken because, as she told me, she'd had a special bond with Molly that was different from the bonds she had with her other dogs, even though she dearly loved them all.

As I explained to her, we love all our animals in different ways, but sometimes during our life we feel as if a particular animal is actually a part of us, and that's because our souls have been together in many physical forms in many past lives. When it's time for one of those animals to go back to the spiritual world and we are still in our physical form, we have to learn to live without our soul mate's physical body on the earth plane.

I also explained that many times, when there is a death of the physical form, animals will use one of the dogs they have lived with to experience living in the physical form again. When that happens you'll see many similarities between the dog that has passed over and the one that is still living.

Oh, Lavinia said, *I do sometimes see Molly's habits and characteristics in Cody.* Cody was a six-month-old male rescue Dalmatian for whom she was seeking a home, and once I had explained it to her, Lavinia realized that, at times, Molly was coming into his body. Now she was worried because she didn't have the resources to keep another dog, but if Molly was going into Cody's body, she didn't want him to go.

She also had another Dalmatian named Jasper, whom she said she could find a good home. If she did that, she said, she'd be able to keep Cody. When I tuned in to Jasper, however, he told me that he needed to be with his friend Alice, a female Dalmation, because she needed him to take care of her. Lavinia said she'd already thought about that because she knew that Alice wasn't the smartest of dogs, and she could also feel how close Alice and Jasper were to each other. I knew they'd both be heartbroken if they were separated.

I also felt that there was another puppy in Lavinia's home. She said that was true, and she wondered whether Molly would go into the puppy's body once she had found another home for Cody.

All I can tell you, Lavinia, I said, *is that Molly will come into the physical body of one of your other dogs. Once they've made the connection with us and our souls have been together, an animal won't move away from us. For now, Molly is sharing*

Cody's body to experience living in the physical form, but she hasn't fully reincarnated, so she's not settled into his body on a permanent basis. She's still going in and out. That's why you're sometimes noticing that Cody is doing some of the same things Molly did.

For example, Herman, one of my dogs, used to push his bowl across the kitchen floor while he was eating. None of my other dogs ever did that, and I used to ask him if he was taking his bowl for a walk. Then, when he was done eating, he'd pick up the empty bowl and put it on his dog bed for me to wash. After he died, another one of my dogs used to do the same thing, and it made me so happy to know Herman was still around. I knew it didn't mean that he had actually reincarnated, but my other dog, Sally, was willing to let him use her physical body from time to time. That can happen when animals have lived together and been very close.

Lavinia was very reassured to know that if she found a home for Cody she wouldn't also be losing Molly. *Do you think she'll eventually move into the puppy's body?* Lavinia asked. *Whatever she decides to do,* I said, *you'll see her enter into one of your dogs' physical forms. I can't definitely say it's going to be the puppy, but you'll know once you've found another home for Cody, because Molly will still be wanting to experience what it's like to live in a physical body and have the same kind of contact with you that she did when she was in her own body. You'll know when it happens, and you'll be able to rejoice in the knowledge that she's not going to leave you.*

Rabbit Run

Animals in spirit often come to us in our dreams, as was the case with Flopsy and Mopsy, two dear little rabbits who had lived with Angie, a regular client of mine, and her husband, David.

Both Angie and David loved their rabbits, and when I first communicated with the animals, they told me all about the beautiful enclosure David had made for them outside in the garden. They also liked being indoors, but when they were in the garden they loved to smell the grass and dig in the ground.

The one thing I warned Angie about was that, if she left them in their outside pen, they would begin to dig tunnels, as was their natural instinct. *Oh, Sonya,* she said, *we watch them very closely. We never leave them alone, but in the summer we like to take them outside so that they can be in their natural habitat.* And, of course, Flopsy and Mopsy loved that, too.

She also explained that David had laid a brick floor under the grass so that they couldn't really dig down too far. But so far they hadn't seen any sign that the rabbits were trying to tunnel their way out. I agreed that was a good idea but said that they still needed to be vigilant because at some point the rabbits' instincts would come out.

Then I tuned in to Flopsy and Mopsy again. They told me again how much they loved the trees and grass and said that

Angie and David took them out there all the time. They also told me about all the people who came to visit them, and that Angie's mother had said she thought it was ridiculous to have rabbits as pets. She was very bossy, they said, and even though Angie and David were happy to see her, they were also happy to see her go.

Two weeks later I got another call from Angie and David. Flopsy and Mopsy were missing, and they were devastated. They'd gone on vacation, and David's parents had been taking care of the rabbits. Sadly, his father had suffered a sudden heart attack, and in her haste to get him to the hospital, his mother had left the rabbits in their outdoor pen overnight. Angie and David cut their trip short and got back home the following morning, but Flopsy and Mopsy were nowhere to be found. They'd managed to tunnel their way out, had emerged from their tunnel in a neighboring yard, and were killed by the neighbor's dogs.

The first thing I said to Angie and David was that they shouldn't feel guilty about what had happened. There are no accidents, and the rabbits' souls had completed their work on this earth plane.

Although they were still grieving deeply, Angie and David had already gotten two more rabbits, and this time they vowed never to let them out of the house. At that point Flopsy and Mopsy came through to me and they were very excited. *Good,* they said, *now we've got two new bodies!* And then they started to argue about which of them would be going into which bunny's body.

Look, I said, *it doesn't really matter. They both have beautiful bodies for you to go into.*

When I told Angie and David that Flopsy and Mopsy would be coming back, they were thrilled. They'd been hoping it would happen but they couldn't be sure. So I explained that it might take a while because, after being in spirit, they would have to get used to the weight of being in a physical body all over again. And I suggested that Angie and David call me again in a few weeks so that I could communicate with them.

The first thing Angie said the next time we spoke was, *They've come back to us, Sonya.* And then she went on to explain that Flopsy and Mopsy had come to her in a dream. She'd been sitting on the grass in a beautiful park when she saw them coming toward her. The sun was shining and there was a beautiful lake and she was just thinking what a beautiful place it was when she saw them running and playing together. *I knew they were happy in the spirit world,* she said. *I could feel the love and happiness, and I knew that for a short time they were in heaven. They both came over to me and then they turned around and ran into the sunlight.* She said that for the first time she felt that she'd been healed.

After they'd had the new rabbits for about six weeks, I spoke with Angie and David again. By then they had absolutely no doubt that Flopsy and Mopsy had come back. *It's uncanny,* Angie said, *how they have the same characteristics and they do the same things.* The rabbits had the run of the house, and Angie had put their feeding bowls in the same place that she had kept them for Flopsy and Mopsy. To her astonishment, the two new bunnies knew exactly where to go. *Sonya, it's like having the same identical rabbits,* she said. *Please tell them how happy we are that they decided to come back.*

Taylor Returns

Taylor was a miniature poodle and amazingly intelligent even among poodles, one of the most intelligent breeds of dog, as well as a charming and loving soul. He was also an extremely successful show dog. When Taylor was very young and just learning how to show himself off to best advantage in the ring, I'd often talk to him when he didn't quite understand what was expected of him. Taylor's mother, Dana, is a regular client and a friend of mine who has many show poodles.

Among his many endearing qualities, Taylor was very chatty. He loved to talk to me and often said there was no reason for me to speak directly to his brothers and sisters because he'd tell them everything I'd said. But he was also very sweet, and when I said that I'd like to talk to them directly he would always agree. He loved his dog family and was very close to Dana, with whom he had shared many past lives, but he had a special bond with his dog brother, Sterling. Taylor was also extremely competitive and enjoyed being a show dog, but it's a hard life for a dog—being constantly groomed, traveling all the time with a handler, and spending long hours in a crate—so once he was retired, he was very happy just to stay at home with the rest of the family.

Dana took great care of all her animals, so they were very healthy and lived long lives. But when Taylor reached the age of sixteen, I was tuning in to him one day when I felt that he wasn't quite himself. I told Dana that I didn't think he was well, and she agreed that she'd noticed he'd been hanging his head. *He's telling me,* I said, *that he doesn't have any energy. He just wants to sleep all the time. And I feel some discomfort in the intestinal area.*

When Dana took him to the vet, he told her that Taylor was bleeding internally and recommended that she let him go.

Taylor told me that he knew his time had come because he was already feeling the presence of all his poodle friends in spirit coming forward to help him go over, and he said that he was more than happy to leave his body. He also asked me to tell Dana that he'd try to come back to her, and I said, *Well, you know, you have that choice. When you get over there you can either come back or not.* And I assured him that I'd let her know what he'd said.

The first time I spoke to Dana after Taylor had passed, I could see him playing in a brightly colored meadow with all his doggie friends in spirit. He was really happy in his light body. *Dana,* I said, *Taylor knew he was going over before you knew it, but he also knew that, at the time, you couldn't have taken it if I'd told you.* And she said, *No, you're right, I couldn't have.*

She then wanted to know if he would come back to her, and I said that he'd told me he would. *I can't give you a time frame,* I said, *because there's no time over there, but you will be with him in the physical body again before you die.*

A year later, Dana decided to get a new puppy. When she called me, she was absolutely overjoyed. *I've got him back,* she practically shouted into the phone. *I knew it was Taylor because when I brought the puppy home, every one of my other animals recognized him. And Sterling, in particular, knew it was his brother. He was so gentle with him, and the minute I brought him in Sterling went right up to him and greeted him with such joy.*

He never leaves the puppy's side, Dana said. *The puppy is always cuddling up to him and they always sleep together. Normally Sterling wouldn't want anything to do with the younger dogs who would just jump all over him and annoy him. I'm just so happy that they're back together again.*

The Cat Who Loved to Decorate

Donald didn't have very many friends, but he loved his cat, Carrie, and spent most of his time with her. He booked regular appointments with me so that he could communicate with Carrie and keep up on what was going on in her mind. Carrie had told me that Don was a man of regular habits. Every morning he went out to get his breakfast from the local coffee shop. He always ordered two eggs and pancakes and before going to work he'd always come home and bring her a piece of his pancake. *I like the pancake,* she said, *but I'd like to have an egg as well.* So Don agreed that from then on he'd bring her an egg along with her pancake.

Carrie also said that every morning when he left for the office he'd kiss her on the head and tell her when he'd be back. Sometimes he also came home at lunchtime and shared a hamburger with her, and every evening they'd go out on the terrace, which he had made cat-proof, while he had a glass of wine. Then one day when Donald called me, he said that he was planning to renovate the apartment, which had been his mother's before him and was really in need of updating. Donald had been very close to his mother, whose name was Alice, and she sometimes came through during our readings. In fact, Carrie also told me that she sometimes came in spirit to visit during the day when Don was at work to keep Carrie company. In any case, Don knew that Carrie would be disturbed by the work he planned to do on the apartment and wanted me to ask her how she felt about it. He also wanted me to tell her that he wasn't going to leave her alone while there were workmen in the apartment. He was going to take time off from work so that he could be home with her and make sure she was safe.

I suggested that we tell Carrie what he was planning so that she would feel she was a part of the process. Donald thought that was a great idea and said that he wanted to buy a new refrigerator and stove and put granite countertops in the kitchen. *Oh, I know he really wants those countertops,* Carrie said, *but why would he want a new stove? I know it would make the room look better, and it would never get dirty. But he never cooks anything. He just brings food in.* When I relayed this to Don, he laughed and said, *You know, she's right about that. Maybe I won't do the stove after all.*

Then Carrie wanted to know what else he was doing, and Donald said that he was going to redo the bathroom and put in a new shower so that it would be nicer for both of them. I told her that and asked if there was anything in particular that she'd like to have changed so long as the work was being done. *Well,* she said, *I'd like the walls in the kitchen to be blue.* Donald said that was the color the walls were now and he'd been hoping to change them, but he agreed to paint one wall in the living room navy blue and the rest of them white, and Carrie agreed that would be lovely. By now she was really getting into the whole process and asked me to tell Don that she'd also like a new blue blanket. *No problem,* he said. *Anything else?*

Tell him I need some new mice and new balls, and one of those things on a stick. We used to have one of those but he hasn't played with it for a while. Don laughed at that and told me he'd broken it but would certainly get her another one.

Carrie also wanted a rug in the bathroom, but was happy enough when Donald said he'd get a new bathmat and leave it down for her to sit on since she always followed him into the bathroom. He then said that he really wanted to put down wood floors and wanted me to ask Carrie if that would be all right. *What's a wood floor?* she asked. And when I explained, she wasn't happy about it. She really wanted a carpet, she said.

Donald agreed to just change the carpet, but when we discussed the fact that putting down a carpet could be toxic to animals he asked if I could get Carrie to accept a wood floor and an area rug. He said that he had an old Oriental rug of his mother's that he would put down. So I explained to Carrie that the carpet could be toxic and that it would also smell horrible for a while, and Carrie agreed to the floor and the rug.

I was really laughing to myself throughout this whole conversation, which sounded exactly like the way a husband and wife might argue about home décor.

Finally, I suggested to Donald that all this work was going to be not only extremely noisy but also disruptive to both their lives, and that he and Carrie might want to move out temporarily while it was being done. He thought that was a great idea and asked me to let Carrie know they'd be living someplace else during the construction, and when they returned everything would be beautiful and new.

All went well and they both loved their new space. It was about a year later when Donald called to let me know that Carrie, who was by now about twenty years old, was really failing. She had kidney problems and was having difficulty breathing, and Donald knew that he had to put her down. *I don't want to let her go,* he told me, *but I can't watch her suffer. She's given me all these years, and I just can't do that to her.*

He was heartbroken and wanted to know how I felt about it. I told him that if she were my cat I would put her to sleep. *That's good enough for me,* Don said. *Will you please tell her that I'm going to help her to go on.*

When he called me a few months later, Carrie came through with Donald's mother, who had taken her over. *I knew she'd be with my mom,* he said. And his mother asked me to tell him that they both came to visit with him all the time. Don said he knew that. *My life will never be the same without Carrie,* he said. *But after she passed I went to bed one night and I was crying. Eventually I fell asleep, and I was awakened by her meowing. I shot straight up in bed, and I saw a vision of Carrie and my mother at my feet. It was only a couple of seconds, but I could feel her weight on my body and it made me know that she was still around me. I hadn't been sleeping well, but after that I fell into the most peaceful sleep I'd had since she passed. I still miss her physical body, but the pain of losing her is no longer so bad.*

Letting Go and Getting Back

Sometimes knowing that your pet will come back can be the catalyst that allows you to let go. David called me when his twelve-year-old Rhodesian ridgeback, Miranda, was diagnosed with cancer. He was absolutely heartbroken, telling me that she was his best friend and that he had never loved another human as much as he loved Miranda. His girlfriend, Tammy, was also on the phone, and she totally agreed. *He loves her more than he loves me,* she said, *but I understand. It's actually one of the things I love about him.*

I don't know how I'm going to cope when she goes, David said. *We've never been separated. She's never been left alone. The day I got her she slept on my bed, and she's been sleeping with me ever since.*

I could tell that it was close to her time, and I told David that I was going to tune in to Miranda. She came through at once and asked me to tell David that she was going to come back to him. *Oh, please, please,* he sobbed. *Tell her to come back. Will she really come back?*

I assured him that she would and that she was telling me she'd come back very quickly. *You do know that she's very close to going, don't you?* I asked. *I'm feeling that her time is very close, but she's heavily medicated and she's not in any pain.*

David said he knew that, and that he hadn't wanted to put her through chemotherapy at the age of twelve. I told him that was very unselfish of him, and that he must remember that our physical body is just the vehicle we travel in when we're on earth. There is no death; there is no separation; we're all connected through energy. He said he knew that but he would miss her physical body terribly. So again Miranda told me to tell him to get a dog very quickly because as soon as he did she would come back within a week.

After that, David phoned me every day until Miranda died. He didn't want to euthanize her, and I could tell that she wasn't in pain, but she was already beginning to go in and out of her body. Finally David decided to have the vet come and put her to sleep. He said that he was holding her, all his friends were with her, and they'd had a lovely service for her.

Shortly before Miranda died, David had told me that he'd spent a lot of time in Italy as a child, and my spirit guides were telling me that he'd been there in a previous life when he and Miranda had been brothers. When I told him this, David said that he'd always been sad every time he left Italy. He traveled all over the world for his work, but he'd never felt the same way about any other place. He asked me to tell Miranda that when she came back they would go to Italy together.

After she died I didn't hear from David for a week. Then he called to say that he'd gotten a ridgeback puppy, and he knew he'd gotten Miranda back because I'd told him that when he did, the pain would go away. And now his pain was gone.

Thea Loves Bubba

Thea lives in New York and is a professional opera singer. I used to talk to her beautiful bichon frise, Bubba, all the time. He was incredibly smart, and she had a tremendous connection with him. He was also extremely talkative and had a great sense of humor. Bubba loved to tell me everything he and Thea had been doing since the last time we spoke. He was very proud of his mother and told me what a beautiful voice she had and how much he loved it when she put his name in a special song just for him. In fact, he was the one who had told me she was an opera singer.

When Bubba finally died of old age, Thea was devastated. She booked an appointment with me to talk to him in spirit, and she said she wasn't sure whether or not he would reincarnate, but she wasn't yet ready to get another dog. *Well,* I said, *we'll have to find out because sometimes they don't. But when they've had a good life they usually are happy to come back.* Bubba came through right away, and it seemed that he was still totally caught up on what was going on in Thea's life—the restaurants she'd gone to, the patent leather shoes she'd bought, and the dinner she'd had with her friends. He gave me all the gossip. Then, all of a sudden, he started to tell me about a new house. *Thea,* I said, *what is this house he's telling me about?*

Oh, she said, *my father bought a house in Connecticut.*

Well, I said, *Bubba is telling me all about it and the renovations and what beautiful counters they've put in and how much he likes the color of the walls.* All of a sudden Bubba had become an interior designer. It was such a joy talking to him.

He also told me about a contractor who had taken money from his grandfather and then disappeared without doing the work. Bubba told me that his grandfather had said the man was dishonest, but Bubba didn't know what that meant so I had to explain it to him. Thea was laughing and saying that she and her dad had been discussing that the last time he'd visited, and she didn't realize Bubba was that smart. *Well*, I said, *he is. Many dogs are. And now he's telling me that he wants to come back. I don't blame him; if I'd had Bubba's life I'd want to come back, too. He said he's sorry that he had to go but he couldn't hang on any longer, and your mother was there to take him over.*

After a few weeks Thea booked another appointment to talk to Bubba. I knew even before she called that she was going to get another dog. So when I got on the phone I said, *Bubba's sitting right here at the end of my bed.* (I'm really lucky to have a job where I can just sit on my bed and talk on the phone and my clients come to me.) *He's telling me that he knows you're ready to get another dog and he's going to come back.*

Just one thing, Bubba said. *I don't want all that hair again. I hated going to the groomer all the time. I want to be pretty, but I don't want all that hair again. And I want to be small enough so that I can be picked up.*

Thea ended up getting a King Charles spaniel whom she called Henry. And she kept telling me that he was a very sweet dog but she didn't see Bubba in him yet. I explained that they don't always go in right away. Henry was only three months old, and it could be a year before Bubba went in. *Right now*, I said, *all you see is a puppy who's barking and demanding and peeing all over the floor. Puppies are hard work, and we forget that until we get another one.*

Meanwhile, Bubba was still talking to us from the spirit world. He was telling me that he didn't want to go through all that puppy stuff again and he was going to wait until the puppy was a bit better-trained before going in. In true Bubba style, he was very funny about it.

Thea had quite a few readings with me after that, and one day she said, *I think he's going in. I'm beginning to see some signs of things he used to do. I think he's been going in and out.* So I explained that it sometimes takes a while for an animal that's been in the spirit world to get used to the vibrations of being on the earth plane. Because the body is so heavy and the spirit is so light, it takes some time for them to readjust to that change.

Thea was really happy to see signs that Bubba was coming back, but then she said, *Oh, Sonya, once he comes back I won't be able to have the conversations with him that I've been having while he was in spirit.* I said that was true, and she would have to make up her mind which way she wanted it, because Bubba was not going to keep going back and forth forever. He kept going in more and more, but it was still difficult for Thea to give up those conversations because once he went into his new body he wouldn't have any memory of his past life any more than we do. In other words, Bubba wouldn't remember he'd been Bubba. We've all had past lives, both animal and human, we just don't remember them. Finally Thea made up her mind that she wanted him to come back, and now Bubba is with her again in Henry's body.

A Hard Lesson Learned

Roseanne was a producer on my television program, *The Pet Psychic,* and we've been friends ever since. Between her and her mother, they had eight Jack Russell terriers, and Roseanne never left home without at least one of them at her side.

One day she called me in tears. She'd been walking two of her dogs, Juno and James, on expandable leashes in New York City. They had stopped at a red light, but Roseanne didn't have her thumb on the control button, and Juno ran out into the street and was hit by a taxi. She picked her up in one arm and James in the other, and a woman in a car who had seen what had happened told her to get in and she'd drive them to the vet's office. Sadly, however, Juno had such serious internal injuries that Roseanne had to put her to sleep.

Of course, Roseanne blamed herself for using the expandable leash because she knew how much I hate them and how dangerous they can be. *But,* I told her, *there's no point in making yourself feel worse than you already do. Yes, those leashes are stupid and I hate them, but you know as well as I do that Juno's time was up and there was nothing you could have done to change that. We all come into this world for a reason, and when the time is right our souls return to the spirit world. There are no accidents, however it might seem to us.*

Still, she was absolutely sobbing, and then Juno started to come through. I told Roseanne that I could see she was with her other dogs who had passed over, and she said that the dogs who were still with her were grieving for Juno. *Yes,* I said, *animals grieve the same way we do. They miss Juno's physical body, but they know she's okay in the spirit world.* And then I said, *Roseanne! Puppet's coming forward!* Puppet had been with Roseanne all the time when I was doing the TV show, and we had made her our mascot. Now she was running all around me. She was an amazing soul, and I loved her as much as Roseanne did. *Oh, Sonya,* she said, *wasn't she wonderful!*

So we reminisced a bit about what a great dog Puppet had been and how much we both loved her, and then I said, *Roseanne, she's got Juno with her.*

Oh, she said, *that makes me feel a lot better. And I do know she's still with me.*

Well, I said, *I wish you could see her in spirit. All your dogs are running around together and jumping over each other. And now your aunt is coming through, and she's got a black dog with her.*

Oh, Roseanne said, *she really loved that dog!*

Well, I said, *she's telling me that she's very happy to be over there with him. And now she's picking Juno up and giving her a big kiss.*

Knowing that made Roseanne feel better, but she said, *I just keep seeing that picture of her being hit by the taxi. I just can't get it out of my mind. And I also feel so bad for James because he saw it happen, too.* So I started to talk to James. I explained that Juno was in a beautiful place, but, of course, he already knew that because animals do. *Roseanne*, I said, *he knows, and he can feel Juno when she comes to be around you.* He just wondered why he couldn't see her physical body anymore, so I explained to him *that the physical body is just a vehicle we all travel in for a while, and then, when it's time, we go home to the spirit world. And we do that many, many times over many lifetimes.* That seemed to make sense to James because he told me that he could feel Juno around him but he couldn't see her; she didn't look the same. I told him that was absolutely right. When you and the other dogs feel her, she's there, but it's different. And that made all the dogs, including James, feel very calm.

Oh, Sonya, Roseanne said, *it's just so hard learning to live without them.* And of course I understand that. *You've had to do it many times, Roseanne*, I said, *and so have I. But the one thing no one can ever take away from you is the wonderful memories you have of your time together. Juno is around you, she's with you, and she says that you're talking to her.*

That's right, she said. *I do, because I feel her around me all the time.*

Then, a few weeks later, Roseanne called me again. She'd gotten a new puppy, and I could hear the joy in her voice. *I think I've got her back,* she said. *Could you see if it's really her?*

Oh, Juno? I said. *No,* Roseanne said. *Puppet!*

Oh, Roseanne, I said, *I'm so happy for you.*

Then she started to tell me that when she got the puppy she was wondering whether any of her dogs would go into his body. Very soon she began to notice that he was doing things only Puppet had done. Puppet used to stand on her hind legs and her front paws would go up and down, almost as if she were walking, and the puppy had started to do that within two days of her bringing him home. And Puppet also used to butt Roseanne with her head, so when the puppy started to do that, too, she knew that Puppet had come back.

You know, Roseanne, I said, *the relationships we have with the animals we love so much are never over. There aren't any ends, only new beginnings.*

SIX

Why Did This Happen to My Pet?

When a loved one dies accidentally, suddenly, or too soon, it is always more difficult to comprehend and accept than when someone dies after a long, full life. And since, for those of us who love them, our animal companions *always* die too soon, losing one to an accident or an illness before their time is particularly devastating. But even when an animal's death seems premature, it has come for a reason, at the proper time for the soul that is leaving its body. It's we who are left saying *he died too soon,* but for the one who is crossing over it is never too soon.

When Jack contacted me right after his Lab, Boomer, was hit by a car, he was absolutely shattered. He told me that they'd been running in the woods as they did every day, and Boomer was off leash, as always. He always came back when Jack called him, but on this day he must have been distracted, probably chasing after a squirrel, and Jack didn't realize how close they were to the road. He heard a squeal of brakes and, as he told me, his heart almost stopped beating. It probably took only seconds for him to race to the road, but it felt as if time were standing still, and when he burst through the trees, there was Boomer, lying right in front of a delivery truck, and the truck driver was pacing back and forth beside himself, shouting over and over, *He just ran in front of me and I couldn't stop in time. Oh my God. I couldn't stop!*

Now, as we were speaking, Jack kept repeating, *It was all my fault. I shouldn't have let him off the leash. I should have realized we were too close to the road. It was all my fault. I'll never forgive myself!*

First of all, I was able to assure Jack that Boomer had died instantly. Boomer was telling me that he had gone out of his body immediately, so he hadn't had to lie there in pain. And then I tried to explain that Jack had to stop blaming himself, because there was nothing he could have done to prevent what happened that day. If there's one thing I've learned from all the years I've spent communicating with the spirit world, it's that there are no accidents. Each of us—animal or human—has a time to go out of this life, and there's nothing anyone else can do to prevent us from following that path. Boomer came into Jack's life for a reason, and when their time together was up, he also left him for a reason. *I know that's not going to make losing him much easier for you right now,* I said, *but you must stop blaming yourself. Boomer doesn't want you to do that. He wants you to know that he's happy where he is and also that he's still connected to you.*

Boomer said he knew Jack was going to find that difficult to believe, so, to prove his continued presence, he told me about some of the things he and Jack had always done together, such as going to the neighborhood coffee shop and sitting outside (since, Boomer stated quite indignantly, dogs weren't allowed inside). He also told me that Jack had always shared his breakfast, and that he liked the pound cake best of all. And he said that he'd enjoyed the charity walk they'd participated in just a couple of weeks before he died. As I recounted those details, Jack actually gasped. He knew then for sure that an accident had not taken Boomer away, and he was absolutely still a part of his life.

When a Game Goes Too Far

Mary was a great animal lover who had rescued two cats from a neighbor whose cat population had grown to at least fourteen and still counting. The cats were roaming the neighborhood and becoming such a nuisance that someone had reported the neighbor to animal control, who arrived one night and took them away. Before that happened, however, Mary had taken in two of them, had them neutered, named them George and Gracie, and given them a good home. She also had two dogs, and at first the dogs made the cats nervous, but they got used to one another and were living compatibly together.

Then, one day, Mary's sister, Helen, came to visit, and that's when the tragedy occurred. When Mary called me she was sobbing so uncontrollably that I could barely understand her. *It's all my fault, it's all my fault!* she kept crying, and I could see a cat in spirit. I told her the cat was with me, and she immediately stopped crying and said, *Oh Sonya, please tell him that I'm sorry. I'll never forgive myself. As long as I live I'll never get these images out of my mind.*

I could feel that the cat had been terrified and he'd had a terrible death. What happened was that Helen had brought her new dog, Daisy, a boxer mix she'd recently adopted from a shelter. Helen was so happy to have her that she couldn't wait to introduce her to Mary and Mary's dogs. At first they all got along well, but Daisy was showing a certain interest in the cats and would get very excited whenever she saw them. The cats were used to Mary's dogs and vice versa, but neither Mary nor Helen realized how careful they needed to be when bringing a new dog into the mix. They did reprimand Daisy, but she was still trying to chase the cats.

Eventually she settled down, and that evening Mary and Helen decided to go out to dinner, leaving the animals at home. They knew Daisy had been chasing the cats, but it never occurred to them to shut them into a separate room.

I'd had a reading with Helen about a week before, when she first got Daisy, and I knew that she'd had a rough beginning.

She was happy to finally have a good home, but she'd been abandoned and had been living in the wild for about a month before going to the shelter, so she'd learned to hunt and go after squirrels and rabbits for food.

When the sisters got home after dinner that night, the house reeked of urine, the furniture had been ripped to pieces, and there was blood everywhere. Daisy must have started to chase the cats, and Mary's dogs, thinking it was a great game, had joined in. Gracie, who was less skittish, had stood her ground, and the dogs lost interest so she was able to go and hide. George was scared and started to run. The more he ran the more the dogs chased him. The more they chased, the more excited they became, until what had started as fun turned into aggression. It was Daisy who finally caught and killed him. Although it isn't common, it does sometimes happen that when a new dog comes into the house, the dog will kill a cat or act aggressively toward another dog. You need to be aware that this can happen, especially if the new animal is a rescue dog and you don't know its history.

When Mary and Helen came home from dinner that night, Mary's dogs were there, but they couldn't find Daisy.

Eventually they discovered her under the bed with the dead cat. George was all wet, and it seemed that Daisy had been licking him in order to revive him. Mary and Helen were both on the phone sobbing as they told me all this.

I just can't even look at Daisy, Helen said. *I know she's remorseful. She knows she's done wrong. She keeps sticking by me and then she goes under the bed and whimpers, but I just don't think I'll ever feel the same way about her again.* I told Helen that she had to learn to forgive and just understand that she could never let Daisy near a cat again.

And Mary said that she couldn't stand even to walk into the bedroom. *What you have to do,* I said, *is change the room completely. Take the carpet out to change the energy and put down a different kind of floor. Replace the bed and just make the room look completely different.* Mary said she really wanted to move but that simply wasn't an option. I cleared the energy for her, and she said that she'd make the changes I suggested.

Both Helen and Mary kept asking me *Why? Why did this happen?* I told them that Daisy and George must have had some issue in a past life that they needed to work out in this life. *But,* I said, *usually when something like this happens, something good will come of it.*

Oh, Sonya, Mary said, *Helen and I have never been this close. This tragedy has really brought us together. We've had our arguments and our differences but we've never had what I would call a close and loving relationship. We've never been openly affectionate with one another, but now we just hold each other and cry. I would never have imagined that this would happen.*

As Mary was telling me this, George came through along with a woman I felt had died of cancer. *Oh,* the sisters both said, *That's our mom!* And I could see that their mother was holding George in her arms, and there were three other cats with her as well. She wanted her daughters to know that she had been happy to get out of her body and that the three cats had been there to meet her. One was black, one was striped, and the third one was ginger. *Oh,* they said, *that's Blackie. The white one is Sam, and the ginger one we used to call Happy.* All of a sudden they were so excited.

Well, I said, *Happy is crawling all around your mother's legs.*

Oh, they cried, *she used to drape herself around Mom's neck and Mom would just walk around that way doing the housework with the cat around her neck.*

And, I said, *she's got the one that just passed over and she's kissing him on the head.*

Thank you, thank you, Helen and Mary both cried. *You've made us feel so much better.*

No, I said, *it's not me. I just receive and deliver the messages. You're getting your joy from your mother. She's thrilled to be talking with you, and she's saying, "Everyone thinks that I'm dead, but I'm not. My body might be, but I'm here."*

Then their mother said, *Tell them that I know they can't get going in the morning until they have their coffee.* So I said, *Your mom is telling me that every morning you drink your coffee with a kick in it.*

Yes, they said, laughing. *We both love our strong coffee.*

Well, I said, *she wants you to know that tomorrow morning and every morning after that she's going to be with you when you drink your coffee. She can do that even when you're not together because once we're in our energy body we can travel really quickly and actually be in two places almost simultaneously. And she also is telling me that she's got all the cats with her.*

At that point there was a Labrador retriever coming in, too. *Oh,* Helen said, *that was my last dog; I loved that dog.*

Well, I said, *he's in a good place.* At last I heard joy in their voices. Finally, their mom said that it used to bother her when the girls fought, and, she told them, *You'll never be like that again. You'll always be close. This terrible experience happened for a reason. It's unfortunate, but that's how life is. The thing this cat and this dog have taught you is that you have to learn to forgive. You have to be kind to the dog. Animals forgive, and you have to forgive. You have to forgive each other. Your cat did not die in vain.*

What I always tell people is that I wish they could see what I see, because their loved ones, both animal and human, are all in spirit; they're out of pain, and there's nothing but peace and joy over there. When you go over, you won't believe what it's like.

An Animal Reunion

One of the most amazing readings I've had in a long time started when Diana called because her King Charles spaniel, Charlie, had been urinating in the house, and she wanted me to tell him to stop doing that. Well, in my experience, when a dog urinates in the house, it's usually a human problem, not an animal problem, which is exactly what turned out to be the case with Charlie. As I tuned in to him he told me that his mother loved him very much but she left him alone for long periods of time and she didn't walk him as much as he would like. As I related all this to Diana, she said that she didn't have time to walk Charlie in the mornings but she let him out in the yard to do his business. And when I questioned her further, she said that he was alone in the house from eight o'clock in the morning until six o'clock in the evening when she got home from work.

I tried to explain to her that Charlie was not only lonely but also that she was asking him to do something she would never be able to do herself—that is, to hold his urine for ten hours on a daily basis. I tried to come up with various solutions, from a dog walker to doggie day care to paper training, but Diana kept coming up with reasons why my solutions wouldn't work. I was just about fed up and ready to tell her that she was wasting her time (and money) with me unless she did something to solve the problem she was creating, when, all of a sudden, I could see a dog in spirit coming through. She was sending Diana love and telling me that she hadn't lived very long because she'd been hit by a car.

When I told this to Diana, she said, *Oh, Sonya, that was Dixie, the dog we had when I was a little girl. I never got over losing her. I came home from school one day and she was gone. My parents told me she'd run away, but we never really knew what had happened to her. I still think about her, and my mother still talks about her.*

I assured her that Dixie was telling me she had died very quickly. It happened near a church, she was saying, and she was sending me a picture of a white church with a steeple. Diana immediately knew where that was. *That was just about a mile from our house,* she said.

Well, I said, *Dixie is telling me that a man found her body and buried her in his yard. And she's showing me a brown wooden house with a park behind it where people walk.*

I know that house, Diana exclaimed. *That house is right near the white church. I have to tell my mother! She still lives in the house where we had Dixie and would know exactly which house she's talking about.* And then she said, *Spirit works in a wonderful way, doesn't it?*

I said, *Yes, darling, it does. And if you walk your dog, that will also work in a wonderful way.* She laughed and said she would do that, and I told her to let me know how Charlie was doing.

A few months later she booked another appointment, and when she got on the phone she immediately said, *Sonya, you really gave me a kick in the pants the last time we talked, and I definitely needed it. I just hadn't been thinking of things from Charlie's point of view.* And I liked her for saying that. Then she said that she'd been walking him and making sure that he was taken out more often and not left alone for so long. Of course, she said the urinating had stopped, as I knew it would. And she also said that while she'd been walking Charlie she had been losing weight, which also made her happier.

And then she said, my mother's here, too, and she wants to

speak to you. So I said hello to her mother, who thanked me for telling them what had happened to Dixie, and then told me another amazing story. After Diana told her about Dixie, she said, she began to wonder if she should go to the house where she was buried and see if the same people still lived there. *So,* she said, *one Sunday I walked over and rang the bell. I felt really stupid, but I did it. A very nice man answered the door, and I said, "You may think I'm crazy, but I wanted to ask you if you've lived here a long time." He said that he had, so I then said, "A number of years ago did you find a dead dog by the church?" So he just looked at me and said, "I think you'd better come in for a minute." He said he did find a dead dog, that it was a black-and-white dog and he buried it next to his own dog in the backyard. He introduced himself as Joseph and said that his dog, Lola, had died just a couple of months before then. When he buried Dixie he told Lola that she wasn't going to be alone anymore because he was putting a friend right next to her. "You may think I'm stupid," he said, "but my wife and I really loved our animals." And then he asked how I knew where Dixie was.*

At that point I said again, "I know you're really going to think I'm crazy now," and I told him how you had communicated with Dixie and told Diana where she was. I couldn't believe it when, instead of rolling his eyes, he said, "Oh, Sonya Fitzpatrick. My wife and I loved her. We never missed any of her shows!"

Then he took me to the place where the two dogs were buried, and there were beautiful roses growing near their graves. He said that he'd planted a rosebush for each of the dogs, and then when his wife died he'd planted one for her, too.

I told her that in England we often put in a rosebush to commemorate the death of an animal or a human loved one, and those roses always grew to be the most beautiful in the garden. And then she delivered her last bit of news.

Well, Sonya, she said, *Joseph and I were getting along so well together that he asked if he could take me to lunch one day. One thing led to another, and now we've moved in together. I just have to thank Dixie for bringing us together.*

Since I know that everything happens for a reason, I figured that the spirits had somehow arranged for Diana to call me so that Dixie could come through and facilitate her mother's late-in-life romance.

Keep Off the Grass

Kevin called me because he was extremely concerned about his dog, Butch, a beautiful retriever mix. His lymph nodes were extremely swollen and the vet couldn't figure out why. He was giving Butch antibiotics but they didn't seem to be helping. *I don't know what to do,* Kevin said. *I feel like Butch is dying and he's only five years old.*

As soon as I tuned in, I could feel that Butch had severe

chemical poisoning and he was sending me a picture of the grass and a lake and a picnic table where he said it had occurred. When I told that to Kevin, he was distraught. *My God, Sonya,* he said, *it's all my fault. I know exactly where that is. It's one of his favorite places to go because he loves to swim in the lake. But about a week ago when we were walking there, they were spraying the grass. I waited for them to finish and then we walked across the park. I didn't think about it at the time, but I'm sure it was that chemical that's making him sick. His neck is so swollen; it's almost as big as his face.*

Well, at least now you know what it is, I said. *You can take him back to the vet, but I think the poison is just going to have to work its way through his system. There's no use beating yourself up about what happened. It was just one of those fluke things. And maybe the antibiotics will help.*

Is he going to make it? Kevin wanted to know. I don't ever make predictions, but I suggested that he take Butch for acupuncture, and I also told him that I would put him into my healing circle out in the universe. Whenever an animal is sick I ask permission to do that. I work with my spiritual guides, Dr. Thompson and the great psychic Edgar Casey, who attach one end of a magnetic field line to the chakra at the top of the animal's head and the other end to my healing circle and then beam beautiful healing colors—blues and purples—through the line to help heal the animal's body.

You have to be positive, I said, *because the power of thought is very important. If you're constantly thinking, "Oh my God, my* dog is going to die," you have to change that negativity to positive energy. You have to feel positive because Butch will feel that positive energy and he'll then think that he's going to get better. So we're going to do a healing visualization together right now. I want you to visualize a positive, healing white light pouring into Butch's head, through his neck, and into his arms and legs. Now see it turning into a cleansing liquid going to all his organs and all the poison pouring out. Now see the light changing to blue. Blue is a very healing color. See the blue pouring into his head and throughout all his organs, just as you did the white, and paying special attention to his lymph glands. Talk to the lymph glands, because every organ in the body has a separate consciousness. Tell them that they'll be well and that the swelling is going to go down. See that light staying in his body, and my healing circle will be sending healing energy to him throughout the day and night.

Then I said, *Here's something else you can do. Have you heard of Reiki?* Kevin said he hadn't, so I explained that it was all about healing touch. *Put your hands on Butch,* I said, *and before you do, ask God for healing energy to work through you. Do that a few times a day. You can't hurt him but you can help him heal, and I'll also continue to work with my healing circle.*

Afterward Kevin said, *You know, Sonya, I've never done anything like this before, but it just feels so right.*

Well, I said, *this is part of your learning, too, and when the time is right, the teacher will be there. So continue to do what we've been doing and let me know how Butch is getting along.*

Several days later, I got an e-mail from Kevin saying that

all the swelling had gone down and Butch was well on his way to recovery. Although he didn't live into old age, Butch did stay in his physical body for another three years, which Kevin always considered a great bonus. And now Kevin has also become quite a good healer himself.

The Cat Who Ran Away

Debbie had two beautiful Siamese cats named Sophie and Clarence. She loved them very much and told me that she thought of them as her "children in fur coats." She was devastated when Clarence got out of the house one day when workmen came to install new countertops in the kitchen while she was at work and they left the back door open. Debbie thought she'd shut both cats in the bedroom, but she said that Clarence must have gotten out without her realizing it when she went back in to get her car keys. Both Sophie and Clarence had always been indoor cats, and Debbie was distraught as she searched and searched but couldn't find Clarence.

Both cats were declawed. That meant Clarence would be completely defenseless in an environment that was completely foreign to him. Debbie was crying as she told me that she'd always been so careful and didn't believe he would ever get out of the house. Now she had no idea if he was dead or alive.

As I tuned in, I could feel that Clarence had jumped the wooden fence in her yard and gone to the right. I could see the world through his eyes, and I could feel that he'd gone down a slope. I could smell the grass as he did, and I began to feel a certain sense of freedom from him. I also felt that he'd gone much farther than Debbie thought he had. She told me she'd put up flyers around the neighborhood, and I said that was certainly a good idea because if people see the flyers and they care about animals they'll be on the lookout. But Clarence had been gone for four days and she hadn't yet received word of any sightings.

I began to receive telepathic images from him, and I could feel with my body the direction he'd gone in. It's as if I were in his body, and I was able to tell Debbie that he was alive. I also felt that he was under a wooden deck or a porch and wouldn't come out. When a cat is lost it will stay hidden. Even if you call it, it won't come out. However, Clarence was telling me that he'd crossed a road. I could smell gasoline and feel the hard surface under my feet. Also, he sent me a picture of a large black Labrador, and I felt tremendous fear from him. He was running as fast as he could, and the dog was chasing him.

I told this to Debbie, and she said she knew exactly what dog I was talking about because he was always escaping from his yard. *Fortunately,* I said, *Clarence was able to outrun him. He's run much farther than you thought. He's in an older subdivision. I can see one- and two-story brick homes.* I also saw the color gray on a two-story house and I knew it had been recently painted because I could smell the fresh paint. Clarence was under the deck. There was no fence at the back but there was a water fountain. At night he would come out and drink from the fountain and then go back under the deck. He was literally eating bugs. He'd never had to hunt, so he didn't know how to do that.

I received a picture of a beautiful bowl, and Clarence told me that Debbie had changed his bowl very recently and he loved the paw prints on it. He also told me he had one particular big mouse toy at home that he carried around in his mouth. *Oh my God,* Debbie said. *He does do that. He loves that mouse.*

I always find it interesting that when animals are lost they tell me things about their home, because they really want to get back home. Clarence asked me if I was a cat, and I told him I was a cat but I was also a human, and that cats had taught me their language when I was very young. I felt him relaxing then, and I heard him laugh. He knew that Debbie had come to me to try to find him.

I was able to tell Debbie that Clarence was at least a mile away, that he was in a yard with no fence, and that the ground sloped down and backed onto a drainage ditch. I also knew there was gray paint on the house. I told her that she needed to go out and look for him, and that it might take some time. I also told her there was a fence on the house to the left as he was facing the ditch. And I said that she'd know the house when she found it, but even if he heard her calling him, he wouldn't come out. *He's in a completely foreign environment,* I said, *and he's reverting back to his natural survival instincts.*

I told her to take a no-kill trap with food in it and also to collect some of her urine, and when she found the house to sprinkle it around the deck so that Clarence could smell her natural scent. *And,* I said, *now he's telling me that sometimes you give him tuna, and he loves it, so you need to take tuna when you go and also take some dry food. And when you find the house you need to sit there at night for a couple of hours because that's when he feels safest. Take a piece of your clothing that's really dirty and smelly and put it in the trap with the dry food and the tuna. And don't expect to catch him right away.* I also told her to let me know when she'd found the house.

A week later I got an e-mail from her saying that she'd found the house and the people who lived there had seen Clarence and were putting dry food out for him. She'd asked them if they could take a picture so she could be sure it was Clarence, and it definitely was him. That in itself was a tremendous break-through. They'd set the trap, and they caught a tabby; they caught a raccoon; they caught a possum, but so far they hadn't caught Clarence. Debbie sat out at night calling him, but he hadn't come out. I just told her to be patient and not do any-thing that would scare him even more. I also said that the more familiar he became with his location the more likely he would be to come out.

The next time Debbie phoned me I told her not to feed him for two or three days and to tell the people who lived in the house not to feed him either so that when she did feed him again he'd be more likely to come out because he'd be very hungry. She didn't really want to do that, so I said, *Do you want to get your cat back or not?* I said that since Clarence was used to seeing the trap and was now more familiar with his environment, he'd probably come out pretty quickly when he got hungry enough. Finally, Debbie agreed.

On the third night, I set my alarm and got up just as it was beginning to get light. I started to communicate with Clarence, encouraging him and telling him it was all right, he could do it, I was with him, and he needed to get that food before some other animal got it. I felt him come out, and then I felt hemmed in, and I thought he was in the trap.

A bit later, as I was having my coffee I could feel a great deal of fear from him. He was telling me that there was a big dog outside the cage. But I felt confident that the people in the house would find him, so I sent him messages of calm and confidence. And soon I felt a sense of relief from him. The people had come out and chased the dog away. An hour later I got a call from Debbie telling me that she had Clarence.

Sadly, however, two or three weeks later, I got another call. Debbie's mother was staying with her and had left the door open when she went to put out the trash. Clarence, who'd now had a taste of freedom, escaped again. You'd think that after all he'd gone through he wouldn't want to go out ever again, but that isn't always the case.

This time Clarence didn't come through, and I had to tell

Debbie that I didn't think he was alive. He'd apparently gone to the left instead of the right and been attacked by a dog. All I could think was that if he'd had his claws he'd have been able to climb a tree and get away. Declawing is not only extremely painful, but also prevents cats from being able to defend themselves if they ever go out or get out by mistake. Many people believe that if they declaw their cat the cat will not get out, but, sadly, that simply isn't true.

Now I communicate with Clarence in spirit. And when Debbie asked, he let me know that he certainly didn't blame her for what had happened, but he was happy and at peace in the world of spirit and he wasn't going to reincarnate.

Labrador Lost

When Jenny phoned, I immediately saw two yellow Labs in front of me, and I could feel that one of them was in the spirit world. In tears, Jenny said, *Yes, that was Bruno. He was shot. The other one is Lucy, and I don't know where she is, but I'm so happy to know that she's still alive.*

The dogs were telling me that they were allowed to run free every day, and again, Jenny confirmed that was true. *I always let them out in the morning,* she said, *but they always came back.*

I know that many people who live in the country do this,

but while their animals are out, they have no idea where they are and certainly wouldn't know if they were in any kind of trouble. Bruno was telling me that he'd been running very fast when he fell down and couldn't get up again.

When neither Bruno nor Lucy came home that day Jenny's husband went out whistling and looking for them. Finally he heard Bruno bark, and he carried him back to his truck and took him to the vet. Bruno told me that he had been in the hospital for a few days, but, as Jenny explained, he'd had a bad reaction to the anesthesia he'd been given and didn't make it.

Jenny was blaming the vet, but, as I explained to her, Bruno's time on earth was up; it was time for him to leave his physical body, and there was nothing anyone could have done to change that. She also wanted Bruno to tell her who had shot him so that she could confront the person who'd killed her dog. But, again, I had to explain that, first of all, by letting her dogs run on other people's property, she was putting them at risk, and second, that Bruno had been shot, fallen down, and never even known he'd been shot, much less who had done it.

As we were speaking, Jenny's mother also came through and told me that she and Bruno were together. She also started to tell me about a particular skirt of hers that Jenny now wore. *That's right,* Jenny exclaimed, *I wear it all the time, and every time I do, it makes me feel happy.*

Well, darling, I said, *your mother is telling me that you look better in it than she did. And she's also telling me she and Bruno sit in a brown leather chair right by the window in your house.*

— 121 —

Oh, Jenny said, *that's the chair my husband always sits in. It used to be Bruno's favorite chair.*

And she'd better tell that husband of hers not to sit on us, her mother chimed in, laughing.

Jenny was feeling a bit better by then, but she was still distraught about the fact that Lucy was also missing. I tuned in to her and felt that she'd run quite a long distance. *She's in a small town not far from where you found Bruno,* I told Jenny. *I can see a McDonald's on the corner, and it's close to an antique shop and a little café with gingham curtains in the window.*

Oh, Sonya, Jenny said, *I know exactly where that is.*

Well, I said, *I'm feeling that Lucy is around that town and someone is feeding her. She also sleeps on a porch of an older, wood-shingled house. And there's also a small black dog that she plays with. Since you know where the town is, I think that if you put up flyers you'll get a response. Just make sure they're big enough for people to see and that they're in places where there's a lot of traffic.*

Jenny thanked me profusely and said that she and her husband would do that immediately. A couple of days later she phoned to say that she had Lucy back. She'd received a phone call from a woman who said she'd been feeding a dog that looked exactly like the one on the poster. When Jenny and her husband arrived to pick Lucy up, they discovered that the woman also had a small black dog who ran up with Lucy to greet them.

I told Jenny I was truly happy to hear that, but I couldn't

help admonishing her about not having had a collar with her phone number on the dog. If people find a dog with a phone number on its collar, they'll probably call that number immediately. If the dog has no identification, they don't know whom to call and, especially in the country, they're likely to think that the dog has been abandoned by its owner.

A Moment in Time

Lionel is a very special person. As soon as I picked up the phone to speak with him I could feel his energy, and I liked what I felt. He told me that he was living in the Colorado mountains, more or less as a recluse, with his four rescue dogs—two black Labs named Hattie and Harold, a black standard poodle called Sarah, and a Jack Russell named Soldier—as well as a wolf dog he'd found wandering alone in the mountains when he was walking the others. He'd taken her home and named her Bella. I felt that Soldier and Sarah were particularly close, and Lionel said that they were inseparable and always slept together.

I could also see that two more of his dogs were in the spiritual world. One of them looked like a Rottweiler and the other appeared to be a German shepherd dog or a shepherd mix. Lionel confirmed that I was correct on both counts. The shepherd, he said, was named Red and the Rottie was Max. Red and Max were both talking at once, and as they were talking I could also hear piano music. Red and Max told me that Lionel was a songwriter.

Then I could see a very bright white light surrounding a young woman coming toward me in spirit. I knew she had been Lionel's wife, Jill. I could see very clearly that she had long, dark hair, was very slim, and was wearing blue jeans and a white top. She was showing me that she'd died when her car hit a tree and then burst into flames. I told Lionel that Red and Max were with her in the spirit world, and she then asked me to tell him that their time had been up; it was meant to be, and he needed to get on with his life. The dogs had been in the car with her when it crashed, and they had all gone together.

As I conveyed this information, there was silence on the other end of the line, and I could feel Lionel's sadness. *The dogs are with her,* I said, *and she's so at peace. She wants you to know that. I wish you could see them as I do, and I wish you could feel their joy and peace.*

I know, Lionel said, *and I thank you, but that still doesn't ease the pain. I had so much happiness with her, and I bought her that white top she was wearing when she died. It was pouring when she left. The car skidded on the road and crashed into the tree. I know I need to move on, but I still find it so difficult. I sold the house we lived in together because there were just too many painful memories and moved up here to the mountains. I can find a certain degree of peace up here with my dogs. If it weren't for them I don't think I'd still be alive. I've thought of taking my own life, but I just couldn't do that to them. Please just tell Jill that I love her.*

But Lionel, I said, *your dogs are telling me that they see her all the time. She's in the house with you, and the dogs are always looking at her.*

You know, Sonya, he said, *I sometimes notice that they just tear off as if they're following someone, and I know it's Jill they're following. I do know that she's with us.* And for the first time I heard him laugh. *The other night one of them took off, and one of the others who had been fast asleep suddenly sat straight up and went tearing after him. I knew then that she was paying them a visit.*

Every night, he went on, *I go out on the balcony with the dogs and look at the mountains, and when I do that, it gives me strength to go on. I feel the energy from the mountains and I know that I have a purpose for being here.*

I could see the poodle standing on her hind legs and dancing around him, and Lionel said that she did that all the time. *They all show me a special kind of love. They give me a reason to get up every day. And as long as they're here I'm never alone.*

On our wedding anniversary Jill and I always celebrated with the dogs. We'd all have steak and ice cream together, and on the first anniversary after she died, I did the same thing with my dogs.

Tears were rolling down my face, and I knew that she was with us. The dogs were all around me, and my beautiful Bella came over and licked the tears from my cheeks. Then another one went to get her favorite toy and dropped it at my feet. We were on the balcony and I noticed that all the dogs were looking back toward the den. They were very alert but they weren't barking. And then I could see why. I saw Red and Max in the den; they materialized and I couldn't believe it. And then, just for a moment, I saw a white light, and there was Jill. They were all in physical form and then in an instant they were gone.

You had a vision, I said. *That's what visions are like. I've had them myself. They're there and then they're gone. You wonder if it really happened.* And he said that was exactly right.

Then, he went on, *the whole den filled with such peace. I felt it come through me, and I know the dogs felt it, too. It was a moment in time, and since that day I've felt so much better. It's changed my life forever. When you tell me there's no separation I know what you mean. It was just so quick, and I wish it would happen again.*

Well, Lionel, I said, *sometimes it doesn't. Just be happy that it happened that once. Know that it was real and that Jill is still there.*

Lionel was lucky to have experienced this visual manifestation as proof of Jill's continued presence in his life. But whether or not you actually see a spirit, I can positively assure you that those in the spiritual realm, both animal and human, do continue to exist.

In Search of Miss Kitty

Losing an animal is one of the most painful situations anyone can experience, and looking for lost animals is the most difficult work that I do. It's extremely exhausting, because I have to put myself into the animal's body so that I experience the world from its point of view. I use all my physical and emotional senses, and I pick up all the distress of the human companion as well as that of the animal. And the work doesn't end after an hour; it continues virtually 24/7 until the animal returns—or sometimes doesn't make it back.

Linda and George, wonderful, kind, loving people who have rescued many animals, called me because their cat, Miss Kitty, was missing and they actually thought she was dead. They told me that even if I told them she was in spirit, it would give them some peace. The not-knowing was becoming more than they could bear. Miss Kitty was an older cat, and I could feel the love they all felt for one another. As I felt myself in her body, I knew she was alive. I felt myself running and looking around, and I felt two dogs chasing me. Linda confirmed that two of her dogs had been playing and one of them had chased Miss Kitty out of the garden, where she spent a lot of her time. *Well,* I said, *one lucky thing is that she's a white cat, and white cats are very distinctive. So if anyone sees her they're likely to remember her.*

I knew she'd gone out from the back of the house. I was feeling grass and trees and bushes, and I felt myself in the underbrush, close to the ground. Miss Kitty told me that she was getting older—I could feel a bit of arthritis in her joints—and usually stayed in the yard, but the rude dog had chased her. She didn't know how far she'd gone but I felt that it was about a mile and a half. Linda and George were surprised that she'd gone so far. Then she sent me a picture of a service station and told me that she'd been eating with three other cats. So I told Linda and George that she was very much alive. She'd gone to the gas station on the a corner, and it appeared that someone there was feeding her. George said he'd go there immediately.

Later, my granddaughter, Emily, came over to my house. We always go through my pictures of the animals I've contacted during the week, and this time, when she picked up the picture of the white cat she said, *Grandma, this is a beautiful cat.* I said it was and told her the cat's name was Miss Kitty. *Well, Grandma,* Emily said, *she's at a gas station. But she's not happy. She really loves her family.*

I told her that I, too, had felt that Miss Kitty was at the service station and that her father was going there to look for her. Emily told me that Miss Kitty was going to try to find her way home on her own, and she asked if we could help her. So we spent a bit of time telling her the way she needed to go.

Later George called to tell me that he'd gone to the gas station and the attendant had confirmed that he'd been feeding Miss Kitty along with three other cats. But she and another of them hadn't shown up for the last couple of evenings. *Well,* I said, *I've been communicating with her, and I feel that she's already making her way back.*

I tuned in to Miss Kitty again and told her to travel in daylight and find a safe place to hide when it got dark, and there were more predator animals around who could harm her. I sensed that she understood and felt that she was a little nervous.

A few days later, Linda and George got a call from a neighbor who said that he had seen Miss Kitty in his yard. He knew it was her because he'd seen her picture on one of the flyers George and Linda had put up around the neighborhood, and he said she looked exactly like that. *Well,* I said, *she's almost home. That's really fabulous.* Linda and George were so thrilled that there had been another sighting of her in the neighbor's garden that they started walking around the neighborhood calling and calling her. But cats won't come out when you call them. They just won't. They're not like dogs.

Miss Kitty let me know that she'd heard her mother's voice and it made her very happy, but she was just too nervous to come out of her hiding place. She showed me that she was under a porch, but I didn't know which one. George went looking, but he didn't see her. They set some traps and waited, and meanwhile they booked another reading with me.

I knew she was still around, and she'd been sighted again even closer to home. I told them that I'd work with her again and show her how to get back. Linda told me where she'd been sighted most recently, and that night I worked and worked with her for a couple of hours, telling her which way to go and letting her know that George and Linda really wanted her home.

A few weeks later, I got an e-mail from them letting me know that they had never gotten her back and thanking me for everything I had done to help. But, Linda said, in their efforts to trap Miss Kitty they'd wound up rescuing a beautiful little stray who had become part of their family. It was really heartbreaking that Miss Kitty had gotten so close, but as I was reading the e-mail I saw her running toward me in spirit, and I knew that a coyote had killed her. I called Linda to let her know that Miss Kitty was in a beautiful place, and she told me that their rescue kitten had been starving when they found her. She was now doing really well, and they had named her after me. I was able to let Linda know that it was Miss Kitty in the spirit world who had led the kitten to her and George, and that Miss Kitty would stay with them forever in spirit. *Thank you, Sonya,* Linda said. *We really know that.*

A Little Girl Learns About Loss

One day a woman named Celia phoned in to my radio program and told me that the two family dogs had killed her young daughter Chloe's pet rats, Sam and Franny, and that her daughter was completely devastated. She wasn't sleeping, she cried all the time, and she wasn't even eating. I asked Celia if I could speak with Chloe, and she put her on the line. Chloe told me she was ten years old and that it was her fault the rats had been killed because she should have been more careful about keeping her bedroom door closed when she was at school. The dogs had gotten into the room and knocked over the cage, and when she got home the rats were dead.

Celia then came back on the line and said that Chloe wouldn't even talk to the dogs or have anything to do with them. I asked her to put Chloe back on the line and explained to the girl that it was a game for the dogs. They didn't really understand what they'd done. The rats were very small and delicate and the big dogs were just trying to play with them. *You know,* I said, *you really can't get any more rats, because when you have very big animals in the same house as very small animals these things can happen, and it's much too upsetting for you and your mother to risk going through the same thing again. But I can see your rats in spirit; they're together and they're still with you.*

Chloe just kept repeating that she couldn't forgive herself and she couldn't forgive her dogs. *I just don't want to be around them anymore,* she said.

At that, I realized that Chloe was much too upset, and this was much too big an issue for me to address in the short span of time I had to devote to each caller while I was on the radio. So I told Celia to send her phone number to my web page and we would set up an appointment for a private conversation. I also assured Chloe that when we spoke her little rats would come through and talk to her.

The first thing I said when we spoke again was, *Your little rats are playing together, and you know that they're still very much alive. They're also showing me a beautiful pink bed with fairies on it.* And Chloe said, *Oh, that's my bed. I used to put them on the bed to play with them.*

Well, you see, they can still see you and they love you, and they're telling me they're very sorry that you're so upset. They're also telling you that they want you to be friends with your dogs again. The dogs are really sad that you won't let them in your room because they truly don't know that they've done anything wrong.

So Chloe told me to tell the rats that she would be friends with the dogs again. I could tell that she was feeling a bit better, and I told her that I was going to send her a book I had written that would teach her how to speak to animals.

Oh, Chloe said, *I do try to talk to them.*

Well, I told her, *I feel that you are very psychic, and I know you can do this.*

Celia, who had been listening to our conversation, then said that Chloe really did talk to the animals and sometimes told her that she felt one of them had said this or that. I told her that many children had psychic gifts, but as they got older and people laughed at them, they stopped trying. *Well, I don't laugh,* Celia said.

So I then told Chloe again that her friends were very much alive in the spirit world and that they were always eager to talk to her because she was very special. *They came into your life for a very short time, and they're saying they don't want you to cry anymore and you need to start eating real food again, because all you've been eating is ice cream.* At that point, I could hear Celia gasp, and she said, *Oh my God, that's all she's been eating!*

Also, I said, *they're telling me that you used to feed them on beautiful china dishes.* Chloe laughed at that and said, *I did. I fed them on the dishes that came with the tea set my grandma bought me. I loved them so much. I used to make cake especially for them.* And then she started to cry again, and she said, *I miss them too much! And I just keep on seeing their little bodies on the floor of my bedroom. I can't get the picture out of my mind.*

I know, darling, that's normal, I assured her. *But eventually it will get better. And also you have to remember that they weren't in their bodies when you found them. They were already in the spirit world with all their friends. It's hard for you to let go of their physical bodies when you're still in yours, but you know they're still around you; you can feel it. And they're telling me that they go everywhere with you now, even to school. They're also telling me that you're very smart, but you're not very athletic and you don't like running around the playground at school.*

No, I don't, she said. And Celia laughed at that, saying, *No, she's never going to be the athletic type.*

Well, I continued, *they're both in heaven, and they're telling me that you pray for them every night when they're tucked up in bed with you snuggling up under your pillow.*

By then I could tell that Chloe was feeling a lot better, and she said that she was talking to her dogs again. So I explained once more that it wasn't their fault. *These things happen in life, and,* I said, *you're learning things very early in your life. Your rats have taught you an important lesson.*

What lesson is that? she asked. *Well,* I said, *they've taught you to forgive. When you were angry with your dogs you didn't feel very good, did you?* And she agreed that it had made her feel bad. *So now you've forgiven them,* I said. *How does that make you feel?* And Chloe said, *It makes me feel happy.*

You know, I said, *that's the lesson your rats came into your life to teach you. You have to forgive in life. Remember that whenever something bad happens in your life, and remember that it's your little rats who taught you.*

Celia spoke again then, saying, *Chloe, tell Sonya what you saw, tell her what you saw in the car.* And Chloe said, *Oh, I was so excited. We were driving in the car and I looked up at the sky and in the clouds I saw my little rats in cloud form. They were so clear. I absolutely knew it was them. So I know for sure that they are in heaven.*

Destiny Calls

Often, when people phone me, the first thing they say is that they don't know their purpose in life. My response is always that this is something they need to discover for themselves; it's not for me to tell them. Grace, however, did not have that problem. She is a lovely and generous woman who has devoted much of her life to improving the lives of feral cats. She has them spayed or neutered at her own expense so that the generations do not proliferate, then returns them to their habitat and feeds them regularly. In addition, she has several outdoor cats of her own and two indoor/outdoor cats named Thatch and Leo.

When she called me one morning Grace was distraught, and I could feel immediately that Thatch was in the spirit world. *Oh, Sonya,* she began, *it's all my fault.*

No, Grace, I stopped her right there. *You are one of the most responsible people I know, and this is not your fault. Thatch is where he should be, on the other side where life goes on.*

As I was telling her this, Thatch came through and began to tell me that he used to live in the house, but one day Grace had put him out and wouldn't let him back in. *That's right,* she said. *That's why it's my fault. A new male cat arrived in my yard, and after that Thatch began to urinate all over my house. After a while I couldn't deal with the odor or with having to clean up after him all the time, so I put him outside. I knew he was annoyed but I didn't know what else to do.*

I understand, I told her. *There's nothing worse than the smell of cat pee. But I also understand why he was doing it. He was marking his territory so that the new cat would know he was the one in charge. It made him feel more secure. But Thatch was also an indoor/outdoor cat. Plus he was originally an outdoor cat, and outdoor cats mark all the time. But, Grace,* I went on, *he was born outdoors and he'd lived outdoors for a long time before you brought him in. So he may have been annoyed, but it wasn't as if he'd never been an outside cat.*

I could see that when Thatch left Grace's yard he'd gone to the right, and he was telling me that he'd somehow got shut in somewhere and couldn't get out. When he did finally manage to get out ten days later, he went back to Grace's house, but he was very thin and weak, and he already knew that he was going to pass.

Grace confirmed that all of this was true. A house nearby was for sale and, apparently, someone had come to show it. Thatch had gone in while the door was open, and when the real estate agent left and closed the door, he was trapped. When he got home, Grace had taken him immediately to the vet, but he was already so dehydrated that his organs were shutting down, and the vet couldn't save him.

I should have known, I should have known, she kept repeating.

But you didn't know, I said. *You can't know everything, and anyway, since Thatch was always an indoor/outdoor cat this could have happened at any time. It didn't happen because you shut him out of the house. I know it's very upsetting to think of him in there and trying to get out, and you're not the only one who blames herself when something happens to an animal. Almost everyone who calls me feels the same way. But these things happen, and you can't blame yourself.*

The bottom line is that his time was up. And his soul is happy back in the beautiful spiritual realm. Also, he can be wherever he wants to be now, and he can sleep on the bed with you every night. He's right there with you. You loved him dearly. You gave him a home and a garden and you cared for him for many years. He was blissfully happy to be with you, and now he's in the spiritual realm and he's blissfully happy there. Much as we hate these things to happen, they do happen. It's all about his karma as well as yours, and there isn't an answer for everything. And, in any case, you'll probably find, with all the animals you rescue, that he'll come back to you.

Oh, Sonya, Grace said, *that really makes me feel much better.*

Well, I'm glad, I said. *And don't blame yourself anymore. You've done so much for so many animals; don't beat yourself up. Just move on from this and know that he's happy. He's just gone home.*

SEVEN

Learning to Let Go

Everyone grieves in his own way, and different people have different ways of coping with their loss. And some coping mechanisms can be rather bizarre. One young woman, for example, slept with the container holding her dog's ashes for two whole years, until she began sharing her bed with a new boyfriend. After that, she put the container on the night table next to her, but at some point during the night she would often awaken, grab the container, and cuddle with it. Finally, one night her boyfriend woke up and asked what on earth she was doing. She was embarrassed to tell him, but as she explained to me, she just couldn't help herself. It was only after I was able to let her know, by providing specific details of their life together, that her pet was in the world of spirit, not in the container by her bed, that she was able to let go of the physical remains, knowing that she and her dog were still connected on the soul level.

And then there was the gentle and loving young man who told me that he'd kept his cat's body in his freezer for several months until the electricity went off one day and he had to bury it. That was a first even for me, and I thought I'd heard it all. When I spoke to him, Luther, the cat, came through and let me know that he'd actually been there, watching his body being buried, and that he was a bit surprised when he saw the man bury his favorite blanket with the body. *Didn't he know I was no longer in that body?* Luther asked me. When I told the caller what Luther had said, he wanted to know if he should dig up the blanket, but luckily I was able to convince him that this was *not* a good idea and that Luther wouldn't be needing the blanket in the spirit world anyway.

Many people find great comfort in hanging on to toys, leashes, dog beds, bowls. Some even continue putting out food and water for their pets long after their souls have left their bodies and moved on. Although animals remain connected to the humans with whom they shared their time on the earth plane, they no longer need these earthly things. And we don't need to hold on to earthly objects in order to remain connected to them. Letting go in one way opens the door to a new kind of connection.

Most difficult of all for people, I've found, is making the

decision to help an animal to go on to the spirit world, even when people know that it's time. Every day people call me because they don't know what to do. In their hearts they know what's right, but they just need my reassurance.

Holding On to a Dear Life

Charles had five cats, two of whom were very ill. On the phone he wanted me to tell them that he loved them and was doing everything he could for them. Sam had cancer; he was seventeen years old and Charles was giving him chemotherapy. He thought he was doing the right thing until Sam had stopped eating and Charles had the vet insert a feeding tube. Sam had kept coughing and coughing until he coughed it up, so Charles knew that he didn't want the tube, and he asked me to tell Sam that he'd never do that to him again.

As I told Charles, sometimes an animal may need an IV for a short period of time if his tummy is upset and he can't hold down food or medication, but I don't believe in force-feeding animals, especially when they're as old and sick as Sam.

But, Charles said, *I'm doing the treatments to save him.* And I said, *But, Charles, he's seventeen, you can't go on keeping him alive. Let him go!*

Charles wanted me to tell Sam how worried he was and that

Sam really had to eat. I laughed and asked Charles, *Have you ever been so sick that you didn't have any appetite? Would you want to eat? The last thing he wants to do is eat. He just wants to go over. When animals stop eating it means they want to go over.*

At that point I started to talk to Sam, and Charles wanted to know what he was saying. *Sam wants to go over,* I told him. *He's just hanging on for you. Animals are so unselfish and love us so unconditionally that Sam is willing to suffer discomfort and pain so that you can spend more time with him, but he's ready to go. He's more than ready to leave his body. The right thing to do is to help him go. We should be glad that we can do this for our animals. We can't do it for people, but at least people have the ability to make a living will and choose a health care proxy who will carry out their wishes. Animals can't do that, so we have to do it for them.*

But, Charles said, *I'll be devastated.* And I said, *I know you will, but Sam has already stayed as long as possible. He's just suffering all the time.* And he said, *Oh, Sonya, I didn't think of it that way. I'm really being selfish, aren't I?*

Well, I said, *I know you think you're doing everything for Sam by giving him all those treatments, but he doesn't want to do it. He's hurting.* And Charles said, *I know he hates going for the treatments. He howls and goes and hides. I don't know how he knows, but he always seems to.* So I explained to him that animals communicate telepathically. *When you're thinking it's time to go to the vet,* I said, *Sam knows it, and that's why he hides.*

Finally, he said he'd let Sam go, and I told him that was the best thing he could do for the animal he loved. *You know it's the right thing, don't you? I said. Don't you feel it's right? Trust your feelings.*

Yes, I do, he said, *and my other old cat, Louie, is dying, too. He's just stopped eating.*

Oh, Charles, I said, *you need to put them down together, because if Louie has stopped eating he's going to starve to death. It would be kinder to put them both down.* Charles then asked me to tell Sam and Louie that he'd take them as soon as he could make an appointment with the vet.

I asked Charles, *Now that you've made the decision, how do you feel? Don't trust your head; I want you to trust your heart and your intuitive feelings. I know you're upset, but deep down inside yourself you'll know.* He was quiet for a minute, and then he said, *Sonya, I do know. I need to put them down.* So I assured him that they'd just be going on a journey home, back to where we've all been many, many times.

He sounded so much happier, and he said, *Sonya, I can't thank you enough.* And I said, *Charles, when you do it you'll have a sense of calm and you'll know it's right.*

Afterward, I got an e-mail from him saying, *You were absolutely right. Although I was devastated at the loss, I felt a calmness inside, and I knew I'd done the right thing.*

If ever you're not sure what to do, tune in to your feelings; your feelings will always make the right decision for you.

The Horse Who Cried

It's rare that animals cry, but Cindy's horse, Nigel, was really in terrible pain. Cindy is a longtime client of mine who has six dogs, two parrots, and nine cats, but Nigel was the love of her life. When she called me this particular time it was because she knew his time was very near. Horses have an average life span of twenty-five to thirty years, and Nigel was already twenty-eight. As I tuned in to him I could feel that he had terrible arthritis, trouble with his spine, and his hind legs were giving out. I told Cindy that he really needed her to help him get out of his body. I'd told her the same thing in the past about others of her animals and she'd always taken my advice, but with Nigel it was different. She had such a strong connection to him that she was just finding it incredibly hard to let him go. Of course, when an animal passes over he's out of pain, but the pain of our grief is only beginning, and I let Cindy know that I understood that. *But,* I said, *he really needs your help now. You've shared so much with one another and had such a close connection because your souls have been together in many past lives. You've come back together many times on the physical plane, and the thought of ending that is very painful. Nigel is telling me that he's suffering, but he'll hang on and put up with the pain for you because he knows you don't want to lose him. The pain in his back legs is very severe and the bones in his spine are beginning to crumble.*

Cindy was giving him pain medication, but Nigel had told me it wore off very quickly and just wasn't working anymore. He was suffering and Cindy was crying. She said that in the past she'd always been able to help her animals go over but she just couldn't bring herself to face life without Nigel. *My relationship with him,* she said, *is different from those I've had with any other animal I've had to say goodbye to.*

I explained again that there really isn't any separation. *There are no goodbyes,* I said. *It's just his physical body that's worn out and he needs to get out of it. If you don't help him you're just going to have to leave him in there until he collapses.* Cindy just kept telling me about all the wonderful times they'd shared, and, gently but firmly, I had to say, *Yes, I know. But those times are over now and he's hurting. What will never be over, however, are your memories; no one can take those away from you. As we travel through life we have to deal with loss, and when we have animals we sometimes have to deal with putting them to sleep. I know Nigel is very special to you, but there won't be any separation when he passes over. He'll still be around you and he'll be completely out of pain.*

But, she said, *I want him to go without my doing it,* and I assured her that he certainly would do that, but not until he'd suffered even more. Finally she said, *All right, Sonya, tell him I'll help him.* The relief I felt from him when I told him was tremendous. Although he didn't want to go, he was actually crying from the pain in his physical body.

He told me to tell Cindy that he would reincarnate and come back to her in some other physical form, and she wanted to know what that form would be. *I don't know*, I said. *It could be a dog, but he's telling me that he definitely won't be coming back as a horse. He says he wants to be able to sleep on your bed with you at night and he hasn't been able to do that as a horse.*

Finally, we ended the conversation, and about a week later Cindy called again. *Sonya*, she said, *I've been so selfish and now I feel terrible. I only put him down yesterday, and it was just as you said, he couldn't get up. The guilt is just destroying me.*

Well, I said, *at least now he's out of pain, and he's in a much better place.*

But does he hate me? she sobbed.

Oh, Cindy, I said, *animals don't hate. It's people who hate.*

She was terribly upset and berating herself for not having done it sooner. *But*, I told her, *you'll just have to learn to forgive yourself. There's really nothing else you can do. We all make decisions. Sometimes we make the right ones and sometimes we don't. Up until now, I've never known you to make the wrong decision, and, in any case, Nigel is now out of his pain, and he's telling me that there's nothing to forgive.* At that moment, I could see him galloping toward me with another horse. *Cindy*, I said, *he's happy and he's running, and he's with a beautiful palomino pony. I wish you could see them. It's a beautiful sunny day and they're having a wonderful time together.*

Oh, Sonya, Cindy cried, *that was my best friend's pony, Spirit. We used to ride together, and Spirit died very young of colic.*

Well, there you go, I said. *You can go on torturing yourself or you can let it go. Nigel says there's nothing to forgive, and he wants you to be at peace with yourself.* Cindy said she would try, and I said, *Please do that. I've known you for a very long time, and in all that time you've always done the right thing. It's just that your relationship with Nigel was so special that you couldn't imagine living without him, and many people don't experience that kind of love in their lifetime. Nigel wants you to forgive yourself and think of him running with his best friend, happy and free of pain. Just be joyful for him and know that he's at peace.* And she just said, *Sonya, thank you.*

A Blended Family

Annie lived in Washington, D.C., where she worked for the government, and she walked her collie, Effie, in the park every day. Annie was in her fifties, divorced for several years, and quite content with her life; she had pretty much given up on finding the man of her dreams. Annie called me often to communicate with Effie, particularly when she'd had hip surgery, and very often her previous dog, whose name was Daniel, came through along with Annie's mother. During our last reading her mother had said that Annie was going to find her perfect mate, and that her mother was going to have to work to make it happen since Annie was completely clueless when it came to finding men. Annie laughed and said, *Tell her I leave it completely up to her because I've totally given up.*

Then, a few months later, Annie called again, and as I tuned in to Effie she told me that she'd found a new friend and sent me a mental picture of a black Labrador. I told this to Annie, and she said, *That's right. Her name is Milly, and the two of them love each other.*

But, I said, *she's also telling me that Milly's father is a very nice man and that he's spending a lot of time with you at home. Sometimes he sleeps there, and when he does you put both her and Milly out of the room. She wants to know why you do that, so I'm just going to tell her that they keep you awake and there isn't enough room on the bed for all of you.* Annie thought that was a good idea, and Effie accepted it.

Then Annie told me the story of how she and Milly's father had met. *You remember,* she said, *that the last time we spoke my mother said I'd be meeting the man of my dreams? Of course, I didn't believe it, but here's what happened. I was walking Effie in the park when a big black Lab came bounding toward me. She had a leash and collar, so I grabbed the leash expecting that the owner would come running after her. But when no one showed up, I found a phone number on her collar and called it on my cell. A man picked up right away, and when I told him I had his dog he practically broke down crying, he was so relieved. He said that he'd parked his car and put the leash on his dog. As he was closing the car door, the dog saw a squirrel and took off after it. He just left the car and ran after her, but the squirrel went up a tree and the dog just kept on running. He asked where I was and said he'd come right away.*

I saw him running toward me and let the dog go. She ran right to him and he just hugged her and started to cry. He told me that his wife had died a little more than a year before and it was really the dog who had pulled him through. So that was Jeffrey and the dog was Milly, and now we've bought a house together and we're going to be married.

Then Effie piped up and told me that she and Milly were going to the wedding. *That's right,* Annie said. *Effie is going to be the ring bearer and Milly will be the flower girl. It's not going to be a big wedding, but Effie and Milly are the most important guests. And we're also taking them along on our honeymoon because, after all, they're the ones who brought us together. You must thank my mother, because Jeffrey and I are so happy together, and if it weren't for the dogs we'd never have met.*

After that I didn't hear from Annie again for another eighteen months. When she called the next time, both she and Jeffrey were on the phone. Effie was ill with cancer and Annie wanted to know if it was time for her to go. I don't like to tell people what to do, but I do say what I would do if it were my animal. And I told Annie that she knew in her heart what was right; she wouldn't have been calling me otherwise and she just needed confirmation from me that it was okay.

Sonya, she said, *that's really what it's all about for both Jeffrey and me. We both love both our dogs so much, and they were the ones who brought us together.*

You know, I said, *it's not over, and Effie is just so happy that you met and that you're happy.* Then Jeffrey asked me to please tell her that he had fallen in love with her mother the minute they met.

At that point I said, *Jeffrey, hold on a minute. I know this is a sad time, but your first wife is coming through. She wants you to know how much she loves you and how glad she is that you've found happiness again. She knows the dogs brought you together and is telling me that the world of spirit had a big part in it. She also wants you both to know that she'll be there to take Effie over, and that there really are no goodbyes and no separation.*

Sad as it was for Jeffrey and Annie to let Effie go, they were both exquisitely aware of the many ways the world of spirit is constantly at work in our lives, not only connecting the earth plane with the spirit realm but also bringing people together in the physical world and keeping souls connected.

The Bond Between Emily and Sam

My little dog Sam had been in my granddaughter Emily's life since the day she was born. He'd been tossed out of a truck on the road in front of my house when he was a puppy and his leg had been broken. I rushed him to my vet and over time his leg mended.

The first time my daughter, Emma, saw Sam she said, *You've got Brue back*. Brue, whom I'd named after an Irish king, had been a huge ridgeback whom I'd had to put to sleep many years ago when he was only five years old. Two weeks later, as I was drinking my coffee in the morning, I looked at Sam's back and all the hair had formed a dark brown ridge. I was so amazed that I practically dropped my coffee. Somehow I'd always known Brue would return, and now here it was fifteen years later and he'd come back.

Sam stuck to me like glue and constantly needed attention. He was also the alpha dog after my dog Ellie died, and none of the other dogs, no matter how big they were, would dare to mess with him. He didn't much like children either, except for Emily. Sam was nine when Emily was born, and from the moment he laid eyes on her they had a bond that was unbreakable. He was always by her side when she came to visit, she could do anything she wanted to him, and he wouldn't let any of the other animals get close to her. Emily was his and his alone. It seemed obvious to me that they must have been together in many previous lives.

Emily, as I've said, has the same gift that I do, and if Sam wasn't feeling well, Emily would always know. She'd come over after school and say, *Sam isn't feeling well, Grandma. He told me when I was at school.* And she was always right. I've honestly never experienced another bond that was so strong between two souls. When she was just four or five years old she would tell me that Sam was going to live a long time so that we could be together for a long time in the physical world. I didn't realize at the time how right she was, but in fact Sam lived to be nineteen. He had problems with his heart and his liver and his kidneys, but he just kept going.

This past Christmas we thought he was going to go, but there were no vets open I could take him to, and the next morning he was again running around and full of life.

The week before I put him down, the whole family went to Galveston. Sam had been to the doctor and they'd given him pain pills, but his breathing wasn't good, and they said that he didn't have much time left. One of my friends had a house in Galveston that she said we could use for the weekend. So off we went—Emma and Emily and my grandson, Peter, with their dogs, my son Patrick and his dogs, and me with mine—including, of course, Sam. By that time Sam couldn't walk more than a few steps and I was pushing him in a stroller, but Emily said that he would love being at the seaside. We got to the beach and let all the dogs out of the car. Emily put Sam down on the sand and for the first time in months he literally ran all the way into the water. He absolutely loved splashing in the water. No one will ever be able to take those joyful memories away from us. It was the last weekend he ever spent with the whole family.

A few nights later he was really having a terrible time breathing and I had to take him to the emergency vet, who gave him an injection that he thought would help. But poor Sam had a terrible reaction to the medication and, to my horror, was in more pain than ever. It was at that point that I knew I had to put him to sleep, but I couldn't do it until Emily had a chance to say goodbye to him.

The next morning Emily came over and I called the vet to come. Emily spoke to him and said, *Sammy, you have to go.* Then the vet gave him a sedative before the injection that would stop his heart, and he fell asleep in my arms. Emily and I both had tears streaming down our faces, and she came over to me and said, *I've just seen him running around me, Grandma, and I know our special relationship will never end.*

EIGHT

Is My Pet Angry with Me?
Did I Do the Right Thing?

Lola phoned me because she was feeling terribly guilty about having put her sixteen-year-old Scottie, Tess, to sleep. *I just feel so guilty,* she said. *I should have waited for her to go on her own. But I knew she was in pain. Her kidneys were failing, she had really bad arthritis in her knees, and she was having so much trouble walking. I just couldn't bear to see her suffer anymore. Still, if she were a person, I'd just have continued to take care of her and make her as comfortable as possible. And I couldn't ask her what she really wanted. Do you think she's angry with me? I need to know that I did the right thing.*

Putting a beloved pet to sleep is the hardest thing most animal lovers ever have to do. But, as I assured Lola that day, euthanasia is the greatest gift we can give an animal we love who is in pain and no longer able to enjoy life in his physical body. The first thing I did was to let her know that I could totally empathize with her pain. I've been through it many, many times with my own animals, so I certainly understood what she was feeling. *But,* I asked her, *think about how you would feel if your body wasn't working right anymore, you couldn't ever get comfortable because your legs were hurting, and you couldn't get around because the arthritis made it difficult even to walk. Tess is so happy to be out of that old, worn-out body. She's no longer in pain. She's in her light body. And even though you can't see her, she's with you all the time.* And then I told her all the things Tess said Lola had been doing. *She still has my food bowl, and she lit a candle for me. She put me in a funny-looking little box and she takes it to bed with her every single night. I don't know why she's doing that, since I sleep on her bed every night anyway.* When I said that, Lola was amazed. *I do sleep with her ashes,* she said, *but no one knows that. I haven't told a single soul.*

Well, I said, *if it gives you comfort, that's wonderful for you. But Tess thinks it's very funny because she's still sleeping under the covers just like she always did.*

Oh, Sonya, Lola sobbed. *That's just where Tess always slept, and I was always worried she was going to suffocate under there. She really is still with me, isn't she? You've just given me so much comfort.*

As I told Lola, I know very well how hard it is to put an animal we love to sleep. But it's actually the most unselfish thing we can do for them. Because our pets are so connected to us, they often need our permission and blessing to cross over;

otherwise they may linger longer than they should just because they know we're not ready to let them leave. And if we can help a pet shed an old, worn-out physical body so that its spirit can be free again, that is truly a blessing.

Sometimes, however, no matter how much we love our animals, we simply do foolish things that can result in their leaving too soon. When that happens, I believe there is also a reason, even if we can't understand it. The animal was meant to go at that time because it was part of its path—but that doesn't make it any easier for the person who precipitated its passing.

Sarah, Samantha, and Cleo

When Sarah called my radio program I could hear that she was extremely upset, but once she'd told me her story I was even more upset than she was. It seems that Sarah had a new boyfriend who insisted that she leave her three tiny Chihuahuas, Samantha, Cleo, and Precious, outside because they weren't house-trained and, according to him, they were "unhygienic." Sarah loved those dogs. They'd always slept with her, and now they'd been outside in the freezing winter for three nights. Sarah called me because she didn't know what to do.

Well, of course, she should have house-broken or paper-trained her dogs in the first place, but at this point, that was not her immediate problem. I knew what she should do, and I told her in no uncertain terms. *If you leave those little dogs out in the cold they're going to freeze to death. If your boyfriend doesn't understand that or doesn't care, why would you want to be with him in the first place? How could you allow him to do this to you and, more important, to your dogs? You've got to stand up for yourself and for them, because they can't. If you can't stand up to your boyfriend, then at least give the dogs to a Chihuahua rescue group who will find them a good home. Otherwise you're going to be living with guilt for the rest of your life.*

I just couldn't understand how anyone who loved her animals as much as Sarah did could let this happen to her pets. *You know,* I said, *love is like a fever. You've got a fever now, and once the fever is gone and you start to face reality, you'll live with the guilt forever.*

About a year later Sarah booked an appointment with me. I didn't recognize the name, but she explained that she'd called the radio program and I'd told her to dump her boyfriend. Then, of course, I knew exactly who she was. *Two of the dogs died of hypothermia, didn't they?* I said immediately. *Yes,* she said, sobbing, *Samantha and Cleo are gone.*

You knew it was the wrong thing to do, I went on. *Yes,* she said again, *and that guy isn't with me anymore.*

Well, he didn't go soon enough, I continued. I just wasn't about to let her off easily.

What Sarah really wanted to know was whether Samantha and Cleo would forgive her. *Well, animals don't hold grudges,* I said.

She told me that after they died she had finally brought

Precious back inside, and Precious was still with her. She said she would never get over what she had done.

Your dogs are in spirit, I said. *They're at peace now, but you won't be because you'll never forgive yourself.*

Do they forgive me? she sobbed.

Yes, I said, *because that's how dogs are. They don't see anything to forgive. It just happened to them.*

At that point a woman came through carrying the two dogs. I described her to Sarah and said that I could feel she'd died of a heart condition. *Oh,* said Sarah, *that's my mom.*

Well, I told her, *Samantha and Cleo are with her. And your mom is telling me they're just fine. But they're not going to reincarnate. We all have that choice, and they've chosen to stay where they are. They're happy and at peace now because they've gone to their spiritual home, even if the circumstances of their passing were sad.*

"I Don't Want to Play God"

That's what Melanie, a regular client of mine, said when she called to tell me that the vet had advised her to euthanize her horse, Jack. I could feel that he had terrible problems with his feet and his back. *But,* Melanie said, *I feel that he still has life in him, and I just don't want him to go. I don't think it's my decision, and if God wanted him God would take him.*

Look, Melanie, I said, *God knows that you're capable of helping him go over. And no vet would tell you to put an animal down unless he was absolutely certain it was the right thing to do. Vets don't generally tell you to put an animal down, so if it were my animal I'd take his advice. I know how hard it is and so do you, but you've done it before and you can get through it now. You've given him a wonderful life, but when an animal is in so much pain it's just humane to help him get out of his body. Jack will hang on no matter how much pain he's in, just because you don't want to let go of him. That's how unselfish animals are, but God wouldn't want him to suffer if he doesn't have to.*

You need to ask yourself, are you holding on to him for you, because if you are, I'm sorry to say that's very selfish. And if you really love Jack that much, you need to let him go. Imagine yourself in his body. Jack is telling me that he has pain down the right side of his neck and he can't move his head to the right. Imagine what that feels like. He's also having trouble getting up because of the pain he has in his legs. Imagine how that must hurt. Where is his quality of life? Why would you want him to hang on? You need to give him permission to go. You know that it's not the end. If this were to happen to you when you're old, and you had nothing to look forward to each day except pain, and there was someone who could help you to go, what would you want that person to do?

After a moment she said, *Sonya, I'd want them to do it.*

All you're doing, I said, *is to help him leave this heavy, pain-filled body. He'll come out of it and journey back home to the beautiful spiritual realm where he'll have all the souls waiting for him from this and previous lifetimes, and no pain from the phys-ical body. And there will be no separation. When he goes over you will feel and sense him with you.*

Melanie went very quiet then, and I said, *Look, you know it's the right thing to do. And all your other animals are coming for him. I can see them. They're all waiting. They're telling you it's time to let go of him. He's trapped in his physical body. All the others are in their light bodies. They're happy and they're at peace. They move freely anywhere, and when Jack is out of his physical body he'll be able to do the same thing.* But she was still resistant, so I said, *Melanie, if you leave him too long, he could be trapped in that physical body for another two or three months until he's ready to go, and then you'll feel guilty. I know you will, because I know you, Melanie.*

Finally she said, *All right, Sonya, you've convinced me. When I really imagine all that pain, I know that you're right.*

Melanie, I said, *it's the right thing to do. And besides, I see another big beautiful brown horse coming toward me and he's telling me that his name is Watson.*

Oh my God, Melanie said, *Colonel Watson.*

And also, I said, *there's a cat that's showing me she used to sleep on Jack's back.*

Oh, Sonya, Melanie said, *that was the old barn cat many years ago. They shared a stall together. Jack loved that cat, and he was so careful that he wouldn't even move his feet sometimes because he was afraid of hurting her. She was a dear little tabby cat.*

Well, I can see them all together on the other side, I said, *and they're just experiencing pure joy and happiness. They're still all around you, and Jack will be, too, and when you go over, they'll all be waiting for you. You'll all be rejoicing together.*

Melanie then wanted to know if Jack would come back to her in this lifetime, and I had to tell her that he wouldn't because he didn't want to go through any more pain. So she asked me to tell him that she loved him and that she would help him to go over.

So I said, *You're making the right decision. Tune in to your heart and tell me what you're feeling.* And she said, *Sonya, I know it's the right thing to do.*

She e-mailed me the next day to say that she'd had the vet over and put Jack to sleep, and she wanted to thank me because, she said, *I couldn't have done it without you. I needed you to help me understand the pain he was in and how selfish I was being.*

Sometimes people are just in denial, and it takes some tough love to help them do what they know in their heart is right.

NINE

Will My Pet Be Upset If I Get Another Animal?

Very often, sooner or later, people who have lost an animal are ready to bring another pet into their lives, but, at the same time, they hesitate because they're afraid that the one they've lost will somehow feel abandoned or think that he's being "replaced."

That was exactly the issue on Sue's mind when she called in to my radio program.

Sonya, I'm so lonely without my Ginger. The house is so quiet, and there's no one there to greet me when I get home from work. I just don't know what to do with myself. I try to keep busy, but I'm not comfortable in my own home anymore. I really think I want to adopt another puppy, but I'm just worried that Ginger will be upset and think I've forgotten about her. I don't know what to do. I need her to tell me that she doesn't mind and she won't be angry.

I wasn't surprised to hear Sue's concern. Thankfully, I was able to put her fears to rest very quickly, because Ginger, an adorable, rust-colored, cocky cocker spaniel, came through immediately. Ginger told me that she knew she was irreplaceable but she wanted Sue to be happy. And she understood that having a new puppy to take care of was the right thing for her to do. Ginger had left her physical body almost a year before, and, she said, it was time for Sue to move on.

When I relayed all this to Sue, she was much relieved. *Oh, thank you, Sonya,* she said. *That's just what I needed to hear. I do miss having a warm, furry body to cuddle, but I was so afraid of upsetting Ginger that I just couldn't get myself to do it. Please tell Ginger that I will always love her.*

You know, you can tell her yourself, I assured Sue. *She can hear you. And, of course, she knows you love her.*

Each animal lover grieves differently when he or she loses a pet. Some feel the need to bring a new animal into their lives almost at once, and others, like Sue, may wait a year or more. But the important thing to know is that whatever makes us happy will also make our animals in spirit happy, too.

A Miraculous Return

When Angie phoned me at the appointed time for our session one morning, there was already a black cat in spirit patiently waiting his turn at the foot of my bed. As I began to tune in to him I could see that there was also a Maine coon cat with him. I felt that one had died of stomach cancer and the other from kidney problems. *Oh, Sonya,* Angie said, *the Maine coon is Samson. He passed over three years ago from stomach cancer. And the black one is Smudge. That's the one I was calling about. He passed just a few weeks ago because he was very old and his kidneys were failing.*

Well, I said, *the whole family's coming through.* That often happens when I do a reading, because all the client's loved ones in spirit are so anxious to say hello and deliver their messages. There was also a gentleman with the cats who I felt had died of heart problems. He was laughing and telling me that he was far from dead, even though everyone thought he was. That's something many of the spirits (both animal and human) tell me, because once they've crossed over, they know unequivocally that "death" as we know it is a physical phenomenon that actually frees the spirit to live on. Angie's father wanted me to pass that information on to his daughter, and she said that she actually did often feel him around her.

Then he told me that he was walking in the snow and began showing me a red scarf. The scarf had no meaning for me, but Angie told me that she'd given him a red scarf for Christmas just two weeks before he died and that they had taken a walk together in the snow. *That's my dad,* she said, laughing. *No doubt about it.* But Dad wasn't done yet. He wanted me to know that even though Angie and her mother were close, he and his daughter had had a special bond and shared many secrets. *That's right,* she said. *Mom didn't always understand me, but Dad always did. I'm so happy,* she went on. *This morning, before our reading, I said a little prayer and asked Dad to come through if he possibly could. And please tell him that I feel him around me very often, even when I'm driving in the car.* Of course, that's how we know spirits are around us. We don't see them with our physical eye; we sense and feel them. *And please tell him,* she went on, *what a comfort it is for me to know that my cats are with him.*

Her father was laughing again. What happens when people in spirit come through is that I can feel the joy they receive from being able to communicate with people in the physical realm. At that point he picked up both cats and said to tell her, *They're with me now.*

Apparently Samson and Smudge were getting a bit annoyed by the amount of time I was spending with Angie's father, because they told me to stop talking to him and pay attention to them. Then they started to tell me all about their lives with Angie. She'd rescued both of them, and they never thought

— 166 —

cats could be as happy as they were when they went to live with her. Then they said that they'd moved from a small place to a larger home that had a yard that was very safe. Angie confirmed that this was true and added that she'd let them go out there with her in the evening when she had a glass of wine and kept an eye on them.

Smudge was also telling me that he was a bit more timid than Samson, and that he tended to hide in Angie's closet whenever she had guests. He said that she always left the closet door open for him but that she had so many shoes it was hard for him to find a spot for himself. Angie laughed and told me that, in fact, she had several hundred pairs of shoes, some of which she'd never even worn. Smudge even said that, just a few days before our reading, she'd bought a new pair of red sandals and that he'd been watching as she painted her toenails to match. By that time Angie was laughing out loud. *Oh, Sonya,* she said, *I found a nail polish that's the same color as the shoes, and that's exactly what I did!* She was totally thrilled, and I explained that they were delivering information only she could confirm, so that she would know absolutely it was them.

Smudge also explained that Angie had helped him get out of his body because she knew he was in pain, and he wanted me to thank her for that. Angie confirmed that she'd done that because not only was Smudge in pain but also he'd lost his sight, and she didn't want him to have to suffer anymore. I assured her that she'd done the right thing.

At that point she wanted to know if they'd be coming back,

and they told me they wouldn't. They wanted to stay where they were because they were very happy, but they said they'd be waiting for her when it was her time to join them. Angie understood. *I don't blame them for wanting to stay with Dad,* she said. *In fact, I was pretty sure that's what they'd say even before I phoned you.*

But Smudge and Samson also wanted Angie to be happy, and they asked me to tell her that she should get another cat. Angie had been concerned about that because she didn't want to hurt her other cats' feelings, but that's not how animals are. They want their people to have another animal because they know how much love and comfort our pets can provide. They don't want us to be alone.

Angie said knowing that Samson and Smudge were okay brought her a lot of peace. She asked me to tell them that she'd be going to the shelter that Monday to rescue two new cats. And she told me that once she brought them home, she'd make another appointment for me to talk to them.

Just as she was about to say goodbye, I had a very strong feeling, and I told her that she shouldn't go on Monday. She needed to wait until Friday. I don't know why I sometimes get these feelings, but I do. Angie agreed to wait, and about five or six weeks later I looked at my schedule of readings and saw that she'd booked another appointment, so I assumed that she'd gotten her new cats. I always ask my clients to send me a picture of their pets as a way to help me connect, and when I looked at the picture Angie had sent, I saw that there were four cats, not two.

When Angie called that day she was so excited that she could hardly get the words out quickly enough. *Thank you, thank you,* she gushed, *for telling me to go on Friday!* Of course, I still had no idea why, but it all came spilling out. Here's the amazing story she told me.

Well, Sonya, she said, *I was walking up and down the rows of cages, and it was so difficult to make a decision. I felt as if I wanted to adopt them all. But one of them in particular reminded me of my mother's cat, Sparkles, who had disappeared about three years ago. My mother was totally heartbroken and eventually gave up hope that she'd ever come back. She was resigned to the fact that Sparkles must be dead. She'd never gotten over it. So I went back to take another look at the cat who had caught my eye and asked the shelter attendant if I could turn her over. Sparkles had a very distinctive scar on her stomach from when she'd been injured on one of her outdoor forays and had to be stitched up at the vet.* Sure enough, when they turned her over, there was the scar. Angie could hardly believe her eyes.

The attendant said that the cat had only come into the shelter on Thursday, so if she'd gone on Monday as she originally intended, Sparkles wouldn't have been there. Also, she'd come in with another cat, and the two of them seemed to be very fond of one another, so Angie decided to take them both. She told me she was crying with joy all the way home in the car, and she called to tell her mother that she had to come over immediately. She didn't say why, only that she wanted her mom to meet her new cats. Her mother seemed a bit annoyed and asked if she could come the next day, but Angie said no, she had to come at once.

As soon as the doorbell rang, the cats ran to hide, so when her mother sat down on the couch she immediately asked, *So where are these cats it was so important for me to meet right away?*

Then, suddenly, Sparkles was there, winding in and out between her feet and meowing. Mom looked down, Angie said, *and immediately dropped to the floor laughing and crying. She couldn't believe it! Sonya, I wish you had been here. I've never seen my mother so happy in my life. She said she thanked God for bringing Sparkles back, and I said, "That's great, Mom, but actually it was me who brought her back!" Then she said, "I guess you'd better go back to the shelter and find two more cats because I'm not giving up these two."*

Angie did go back to get two more cats, which is why there were four in the photo she sent. But the story got even more amazing than that. When she told me about getting Sparkles back, I suggested that I would tune in and see where she'd been for the past three years. Here's what Sparkles told me.

She'd been chased by a coyote and climbed a tree to get away. She stayed up there a long time, and when she finally came down she was lost. She didn't know where to go and she had to hunt for her food. She worked out what was her territory, and after a while she found out that someone was feeding stray cats. I don't know exactly how cats find this out, but they generally learn very quickly if someone is putting food out. So she was eating with three other cats this person was feeding, and then one day a new cat showed up. The new cat let Sparkles know that he lived a bit farther away, and he took her back to where he was living with an elderly lady. She then let Sparkles in, so she had found a new companion and a new home. But then one day the lady fell and someone came and took her away on what Sparkles thought was a bed but must have been a stretcher. Shortly after that someone else came and took Sparkles and the other cat to the shelter. It was just the day after that when Angie showed up and took them home with her. To me, that was truly a miracle.

Angie's mother is reunited with Sparkles, who is also still with her special cat companion, and Angie's two new kittens are also thriving, giving her a lot of love, and getting along well with one another.

A Psychic Awakening

When Michael called me he told me that he and his longtime partner, Clive, had lost their beautiful red setter, Lucy, ten years ago. Four years later, Michael said, Clive also died. Michael was still in deep mourning for them both and couldn't seem to move forward with his life.

He said that he'd been in his car one day when my radio program came on the air. He couldn't believe what he was hearing. *Here was this woman,* he said, *talking to people and their pets in the spirit world! I pulled over to the side of the road to listen, and I was totally astounded. I'd never experienced anything like it, and in fact I didn't believe it when people talked about psychics. And all the time you were connecting with animals and people. I said to myself, I think this woman is for real! So I looked up your website and booked this appointment, and last night I was so excited I couldn't sleep. So here I am talking to you.*

I could see Michael's partner, Clive, coming through, and I also saw that Lucy was with him and that there was a beautiful sunset behind them. Clive was holding a cigarette in one hand and a glass of wine in the other, and he was making a toast to Michael. Then he held the glass to his nose and sniffed the wine. I could see that there were crates and crates of wine all around him. When I told this to Michael, he said, *Oh my God, Sonya, he was a wine salesman. That's definitely Clive.*

Well, I said, *he's also telling me that he was a smoker, and although he'd tried many times to kick the habit, he was never able to quit. He wants me to tell you he's sorry, but he just couldn't give it up.*

That's right, Michael said. *He couldn't. Oh, gosh,* he said. *I can't believe this.*

He wants you to know that he loves you, I went on, *and that he's got Lucy with him, too.*

Michael started to cry. *I'm so lonely,* he said, *I just don't want to live anymore.*

With that Clive said, *And don't you try that ever again. You're not very good at it.* To me he said, *He's supposed to be where he* is, and tell him to stay there. I don't want him over here yet. We'll all be together when the time is right, and in any case, we're together right now anyway.

When I relayed that message to Michael, he said he knew that. And I said, *Yes, and if you'd taken your own life they'd probably have tossed you right back anyway, because it's wrong to try to take your life.*

Oh, Sonya, Michael said, *please tell him I won't ever try that again. I didn't have the nerve to take enough pills, and all I did was make myself so sick that they had to rush me to the hospital and pump my stomach.*

I passed that message along to Clive, whose response was, *That was very foolish, but he never did have a lot of common sense.*

At that point Lucy started to tell me how much she loved Michael and that they'd moved into a new house in California with an ocean view. She said that Clive was very handy, that he'd put a new wooden floor in the house, and that she had helped. She also told me that she loved the black granite they had put in the kitchen and that they'd all sat on the deck every evening. Michael and Clive would each have a glass of wine, and they'd also given her a beautiful glass to drink her water from while they were out there.

Michael confirmed all of that, and for the first time I could feel some joy return to his voice. *We used to say, Only the best for you, Lucy,* he told me. *And she loved drinking her water from that glass. Oh, Sonya,* he went on, the sadness returning, *I miss them so much. I never sit on that deck anymore; it just has too many painful memories. I go out and look at the beautiful view, and then I go right back inside and turn on the television.*

I tried to explain to him how lucky he was to have those memories, but for Michael they were just too sad.

Then Clive came in again and said, *Tell him to get another dog.*

When I told that to Michael he said he'd feel much too guilty because he believed that Lucy would be upset. *Michael,* I said, *animals and people in the spirit world just want us to be happy. They don't get jealous and they don't get upset. When we leave our physical body we leave all the junk behind, and both Lucy and Clive want you to get another dog.*

You mean she wouldn't mind? he asked. *Of course she wouldn't mind,* I said. *It's only you who thinks like that, not her. What you're doing isn't living, Michael. You're still in your physical body, and you've got to start enjoying life again. And also, if you get another dog, Lucy might decide to reincarnate and come back to you. So just do it. It's up to you to change your mind, and if you change your mind you'll change your life. Whether Lucy comes back or not, you won't be lonely anymore. Another dog will make you happy and will give you a purpose in life. And if you get a dog from a shelter, it will change the dog's life, too. There's a dog out there for you; you just have to go out there and find it. I'm not saying you'll ever forget Lucy, but after ten years you need to stop wallowing in self-pity. You know, it wasn't an accident that you heard me on the radio that morning. That was meant to happen. And you can change your life in less than a day if you want to. So just go out there and find another best friend.* And all the while

I was saying all that, I could hear Clive in spirit laughing and saying, *Thank God, thank God, Sonya. You tell him!*

Finally Michael agreed that he did want to change his life, and I told him that both Lucy and Clive said that when he went to get the dog they would help him to choose it.

Three months later Michael had booked another appointment, and when he came on the line he sounded like a totally different person. In front of me I had a picture of not one dog but two beautiful Boston terriers. Immediately I could feel such happiness coming through from all of them. *They're littermates,* Michael said. *They were about to be euthanized, and I wouldn't dream of taking one without the other. They were huddled together and I immediately felt the connection. I told them they were both going home with me. I call them Wiggles and Jasmine—Wiggles because he's always wiggling his backside and his tail is always going, and Jasmine just because I thought it suited her.*

Then Clive and Lucy came through, and Clive told me to tell Michael that they were both so happy for him and that they had directed him to the dogs. *I know,* Michael said. *I could feel them, Sonya. When I saw the dogs, I just knew they were for me. You were absolutely right. I had to change my life. And, my God, have they changed it! I'd been living like a recluse for years, and now I've already started to meet people and make new friends, just from taking them to the dog park. I'm living my life again, and now I'm even going to have a party by the pool where people can all come with their dogs.*

Well, you tell him Lucy and I will both be there, Clive said.

Jasmine told me that she was the one in charge and Wiggles was much more easygoing, and Michael said that was true. He also told me that they were in very good condition when he got them from the shelter and seemed to have been well taken care of. Jasmine said that they'd both been well loved but that their previous human companion had been very ill and had to give them up. I then saw a woman coming forward who told me her name was Jill and that she'd died of cancer. She said the dogs had been the loves of her life and that when she was ill she worried more about them than she had about herself. She told herself that if they were euthanized they'd all be together on the other side. And then Michael found them. *Tell him they were meant to be with him,* she said.

And Michael said, *I can feel that, and please tell her that she can come to visit us anytime.*

Well, Jill said, *he doesn't really have much choice about that, because I drop in all the time. The dogs can see me, but he doesn't.*

Finally, Michael said, *You know, Sonya, after I brought the two new babies home, I sat out on the deck for the first time. I had a glass of wine and gave them each a glass of water. My memories were happy again and, for the first time, I could smell cigarette smoke and I knew that Clive and Lucy are still with me. I used to hate that smell, but now I love it.*

Our pets just want us to be happy and move on, so they never mind when we bring a new animal companion into our lives. It's we who worry—not only that the pet we've lost will be angry or jealous, but also that we won't love our new companion as much, or in the same way, as the one we've lost. Our hearts, however, are infinitely expandable. Love has no limits. Your new pet will be different, with his own personality, quirks, and habits, so your relationship with him will also be different, but that doesn't mean it will be less intense, less loving, or less rewarding for both of you.

TEN

Who's Taking Care of My Animal Now That I'm Not with Him Anymore?

I'm so worried about my poor Misty, Jessica moaned into the telephone. *She was a really picky eater and I always made sure to cook food especially for her. She was a Yorkshire terrier with a beautiful, long, silky coat. I bathed her once a week and I brushed her every day. I had a whole collection of bows to put in her top-knot, and I could tell by the way she always cocked her head and strutted down the street that she was proud of how she looked. I loved taking care of her, but who's doing all those things for her now? I just worry about her all the time.*

If I weren't so convinced that Jessica was absolutely sincere in her concerns, and if I hadn't heard much the same thing so often from others who had lost their pets, it would have been difficult for me to keep from laughing. But, of course, I didn't laugh, and Jessica couldn't see me smiling. Instead I reminded her gently that Misty was no longer in her body. She had moved on to the world of pure spirit, and on the spiritual plane, with no physical body, she didn't need food, and she certainly didn't need to be bathed and brushed.

Jessica was still having difficulty coming to terms with that concept, but when I told her that Misty wanted me to let her know how much she'd always appreciated Jessica's loving care, and how she loved all those different colored bows, but especially the white one with red polka dots, I think she began to feel a bit better. Then Misty said she thought that Jessica really missed having someone to take care of, and that she might feel better if she brought a new puppy into her life. There was an audible intake of breath when I said that, because, Jessica admitted, she'd actually thought the same thing. But she couldn't bear the thought of what she called "betraying" Misty by getting another dog. So again I had to reassure her that all Misty wanted was for her to be happy. And that she never had to worry about Misty's feeling she was being replaced. She would always be connected to Jessica, and she understood how important it was for Jessica to be sharing her life in the physical world.

Very often, when we worry about how our animals are "getting on" in the world of spirit, it's because of our own needs rather than theirs. They have everything they need, including their ongoing connection to us, and it isn't selfish to consider our own needs because moving on with our lives is what they truly wish for us.

A Victim of Circumstance

Whether it's a natural disaster or a reversal of circumstances, people sometimes become separated from their beloved pets and never know what happened to them. That was Martha's situation. She lost her home in the recession and had to leave her dog, Harvey, at a shelter. She had no idea what his fate had been or even if he was still alive.

I immediately began to tune in to a beautiful German shepherd dog, and I had to tell Martha that Harvey had been euthanized. But I could see him running toward me in spirit. Martha kept asking, *Does he hate me? Does he know I had no other choice?*

I assured her that dogs don't hate. It's just not in their nature. And I also explained that when they get to the spirit world they are reunited with all the other souls they've known in this life and in past lives. I could see that there was a gentleman with Harvey whom I felt was a close relative who'd passed from a stroke. *Oh,* Martha said, *that's my father.* He was telling me that they'd lived in the country and that he'd taught Martha to drive. I said that it seemed to me he had been a bricklayer. *He was a builder,* Martha exclaimed. *He built our house.*

I was able to tell her that her grandmother was also with her dad and her dog. I could also see that Martha had other animals with her. *Yes,* she said. *I've been lucky. I've turned my life around and I'm married now.*

Is one of your dogs named Teddy? I asked. And she said it was. I told her that I also saw another little black-and-white dog, and she said that was Emmy. I told her that Harvey went in and out of Teddy's body all the time. She was thrilled and said that explained a lot. One of the things Harvey used to do all the time was run around her in circles. None of her other dogs except Teddy had ever done that. She said she'd always felt it was Harvey, but she didn't know that dogs could reincarnate. I assured her they could and that she quite literally had gotten her dog back.

He's rolling over and running away and coming back right now, I said. *And your dad is telling me that your little black-and-white dog is the small one you had when you were a little girl, who had barked all the time and lived to be very old.*

Yes! Martha said. *We thought she'd never die!*

By this time Martha was so happy, but her dad had even more messages to deliver. When he said he wanted to wish her a happy birthday Martha went totally quiet. *It's my birthday today,* she said after a moment, *and this session with you is my birthday gift from my husband. I couldn't have had a better birthday!*

She was in tears, but there was more. *There's a woman with your father,* I said. *I think it's his sister. She died of cancer and she was very bossy.*

Oh my goodness, Martha exclaimed. *That's Aunt Ethel.*

She's got nine cats with her, I said. And Martha laughed. *That woman was crazy about cats!*

You're a lot like me, Aunt Ethel told Martha. *You're pretty bossy yourself!*

By that time Martha was laughing out loud. *Thank you, thank you, Sonya,* she said. *You've finally put my mind at rest. I've lived with this pain for so long.*

It's always so rewarding for me to be able to assure people that their animals in spirit are with their loved ones and are happy, peaceful, and content.

Reunited in Spirit

Melody called because she had recently lost a beloved pet, and a friend who listened to my radio program had suggested she book an appointment. Even though Melody was not at all familiar with my work, she was not skeptical and was completely open to the idea that the physical body is only one phase of eternal life for both animals and humans.

I had in front of me pictures Melody had sent of Luna, a beautiful Rottweiler, Sophie, a small terrier—both of whom had passed—and a German shepherd dog called Tate, who was still in his physical body. Sophie had died two years before and Luna quite recently. I could feel that both Tate and Melody were grieving deeply for Luna.

She looked up to me, Tate told me. *I always took care of her and I miss her very much.*

That's right, Melody said. *From the moment we got Luna, Tate started to take care of her, and now he's so sad that he's not eating very well.* I know that when animals grieve they often lose their appetite, just like humans do, and I suggested that she give Tate some chicken and said that he was also telling me that he liked cheese, but he didn't want to eat his dog food. *Just give him things he likes that might tempt him, and don't worry about the dog food right now. As he starts to get his appetite back, you can begin to add it in again, but dogs are often tempted by things like chicken or turkey and cheese or sweet potato. Those are all good foods, so you really don't have to worry so much about the dog food right now.*

Then Tate started to tell me that he was very friendly and liked to be with people and other dogs, so I suggested to Melody that she take him for a ride in the car to get him out of the house where all the memories were and change his routine. *It will be good for him, and for you, too,* I said, *to get out and be with other people. Also, when you take him for a walk, take a different route, not the one you always followed with Luna. Go to a completely different environment where he won't remember her walking by his side.*

Melody agreed that would be a good idea because, she said, *Whenever we walk where we used to go with Luna it makes me sad, and I can also feel his sadness.*

Finally, I told her not to wash any of the blankets or toys that Luna used to play with, because animals' primary sense is smell and recognizing her scent on the toys and blankets would be a comfort to Tate. Sometimes when an animal companion has passed, the animals who are still with us will go to the spots where their friends used to be. It helps them to feel that the one in spirit is still with them, and it does give them some comfort. *I'd noticed that he was doing that,* Melody told me, *but I didn't really understand why. Thank you for explaining it to me. I might have started washing those things, but now I know not to do that.*

At that point I saw a gentleman in the spirit world coming forward with a small dog in his arms, and he was telling me that he'd died of a heart attack. *Oh, that's my dad,* Melody said.

Well, I told her, *he's got Sophie in his arms. Luna is also with him, and I can see a black Labrador running around his feet.*

Oh, that Lab was my childhood dog, Melody said. *He taught me everything I know about loving dogs.*

I assured her that they were all together and that her father was sending her his love. It made Melody feel much better to know that none of them was alone, and she also expressed her surprise that I'd been able to make contact with her father. So I explained that, because we're all reunited in the spirit world, our relatives often come through because they want to talk to us and also to let us know that our animals are with them.

As I was explaining this, I could feel that Melody's dad hadn't always been an easy person to be with when he was alive. He was letting me know that he had had quite a temper and he'd found it very difficult to express love, and he'd never actually told Melody he loved her; I told her what I was sensing, and she immediately confirmed that this was true. *I never, ever remember him saying I love you,* she told me. *Well, he's telling you now,* I said. *He wants both you and your mother to know how much you mean to him, and he wants you to tell your mother that he's sorry, because he doesn't think he was a very good husband.*

It's true, he wasn't always, Melody said, *but other times he was.*

Well, I said, *he really wanted to let you know how sorry he was and to ask your forgiveness.*

Sonya, Melody replied without missing a beat, *you tell him there's nothing to forgive.*

After that he went on to tell me what a good driver his daughter was. Melody laughed at that and said, *Sure, that's because he's the one who taught me!*

Well, I said, *he wants you to know that he doesn't mind being in the car with you.*

You know, Sonya, she said, *I've often feel that he's there with me when I'm driving,* and I assured her that whenever she had that feeling it was because he was sitting right there next to her.

In the end, Luna also began to talk, telling me that she'd been a rescue dog and that she'd been so happy from the time that she went to live with Melody. She also told me that Tate had always looked after her and that her mother had sung to her all the time. *It was a beautiful song,* she said, *but it was always the same one.*

That's right, Melody said, laughing. *I used to sing "Amazing Grace" to her all the time.*

Luna also told me that she'd died young and that it had something to do with water. Melody started to cry again then, and she told me that Luna had been running and it had been very hot, and she got so overheated and dehydrated that even though Melody had rushed her to the vet, he hadn't been able to save her. *It was a terrible accident,* she said.

Of course, I explained, as I do to all my clients, that there are no accidents. When our time is up, there's nothing anyone can do to change our path, and the same is true for animals as it is for people.

Just then, Tate jumped in and told me that he could feel Luna around him even though he couldn't see her. I told him that was because she was now in her energy body, and I explained what happens to all of us when we go out of our physical body. I also told him that when we leave our physical body we go to a special place called "home" that's a different home in a different place, and I could sense that he understood every word I was saying. He told me that he'd also sometimes seen Melody's father, and that he'd also seen Sophie sleeping on his mother's bed. But, he said, he was still missing Luna even though he knew she was still there. I assured him again that she was, indeed, still there even though she looked different, and that once he was in his energy body, as we all would be at some point, he'd be with her and all the other people and animals in spirit he could see and sense around him.

Back in Her Mother's Arms

Tanya is a lovely, kind lady who has called me for readings on a number of occasions. This time, I could see that one of her two spaniels, Rebecca, had passed into the world of spirit. As Tanya and I began to talk, I saw a woman in spirit coming toward me. I felt that she had died from cancer and could see that Rebecca was with her.

Tanya, I said, *I see a woman on the other side and Rebecca is with her. I also feel that they were together before in their physical bodies.*

Oh, yes, Tanya said. *That's my mother. I asked her to come through in this reading and I knew that she would. Rebecca was her dog originally, and I took her when my mother died.*

Rebecca told me that she'd had a lot of back pain and had gone blind before she died but that she'd managed to find her way around very well. Tanya again confirmed that this was true. Animals do seem to cope well when they lose their sight because they are able to communicate telepathically. So, when we visualize something, as we do all the time without being aware of it, that picture goes out into the energy field where the dog can pick it up. For example, you might think *I'm going to take my cup of coffee into the living room and drink it while I'm sitting on the sofa reading the paper.* When you do that you have a mental picture of the living room and of yourself sitting with your coffee on the sofa. And when the dog picks that up telepathically, it's easier for him to find his way around and come to you.

Rebecca also said that she'd lived to be fifteen years old and that she was afraid of water. At the same time, Tanya's mother was telling me how happy she was to have her dog back with her again.

Tanya was in tears as she told me that one day someone had left a door open and Rebecca had found her way out to the pool area. *She never went out there,* Tanya said, weeping, *because she really was afraid to go near the water. I don't even know how she got all the way to the other end of the garden, but I found her in the pool. I pulled her out, but it was too late.*

Well, Tanya, I said, *now she's out of her pain. She's telling me that this is the way she chose to go and that she's at peace. I can feel her happiness. Also, your mother is telling me that she went out of her physical body very quickly, and they are both so happy to be together again.*

At that point Rebecca started to tell me how much she liked the new green dress Tanya had bought. *But I only bought that dress yesterday!* Tanya exclaimed.

Well, darling, I said, *Rebecca was with you when you bought it, and she's also telling me that you met a friend for lunch and that she and your mother were both there. Plus, your mom enjoyed the shopping trip, too. Over there they can do what they like and go where they like. When Rebecca died, she moved onto another plane of reality, as all souls do. Over there we're free; we're in our energy body.*

Oh, Sonya, Tanya said, *I feel so much better to know that Rebecca is with my mom. I knew she was in pain but I just couldn't let her go and I was hoping that the pain medication was helping her. But if she was saying she was in pain I guess it wasn't really working.*

Tanya, I said, *Rebecca knows all that. Sometimes animals are very smart and they just take things into their own hands, and I believe that's what Rebecca did. Also, your mother is saying that you'll feel their energy telling you that they're both much happier now. I want you to tune in to that energy. Just close your eyes and concentrate for a minute and then tell me what you feel.*

Tanya did that and after a few moments she said, *Sonya, I feel they are at peace.*

Old Friends

Sometimes it can be easier to let an animal go over if we know in advance that he'll be looked after by someone he knew while he was in his physical body.

Maureen phoned me from her home in Northern Ireland. She had two dogs named Lassie and Sandy and had seen me on television when I went to Dublin to publicize my first book. Now she was calling because Sandy was eighteen years old and very ill, and Maureen didn't know whether it was time to put her to sleep. She wanted me to talk to Sandy, and as I tuned in to her I could see a gentleman in spirit who told me he had died of a stroke.

That's my husband, Frank, Maureen said. *He died three years ago. I asked him to come through and I knew he would. Could you please ask him to stop fooling with my electricity. Lights and appliances keep turning themselves on and off, and they never did that before he died. I had it all checked out and there's nothing wrong with the wiring. So please tell him I know he's still around and he doesn't have to keep turning on the television in the middle of the night. In fact, I'm fed up with it.*

As Maureen was telling me all this, I could hear Frank laughing in the spirit world. I explained that because spirits are pure energy it's easy for them to do things like that, and Maureen said that was all well and good but he was aggravating her just like he did when he was on the earth plane. *So please tell him that if he doesn't stop I'm not going to speak to him ever again, and I talk to him all the time.* All of this was said with a great deal of good-natured humor, and I could tell that she and Frank must have had a bantering and loving relationship. They both seemed to have a great sense of humor.

After that little exchange, Maureen wanted me to ask Sandy

if she was ready to go. I could tell that she had arthritis in her back legs, she was having difficulty breathing, and she was incontinent, which upset her a great deal. Maureen thought her dog was suffering, even though she was being given pain medication, and Maureen didn't want her to suffer. I said, truthfully, that she was. The pain medication wasn't working very well anymore, her body was worn out, and it would be much kinder to let her go.

You tell her I understand, Maureen said. *I'm seventy-eight years old. Tell her she doesn't have to hang on for me. She has my permission to go, and ask her if she wants my help. I've loved her for a long time and Lassie is going to miss her a lot, but tell her it's okay with both of us and she'll be going over to see her dad. Just ask him if he's going to take as good care of her as I've been doing.* And Frank, of course, said that he would.

When I tuned in to Sandy, I could feel that she was ready. She also told me that she had the most loving family and wanted me to thank her mom and dad. She also wanted to send her love to Lassie, who had been her constant companion for many years.

I knew that Lassie was already grieving because she knew Sandy's time had come. *Don't worry,* she said, *I'll see you around. We'll be together anyway.*

Then Maureen told me that she'd call the vet to come to the house and help Sandy leave her body.

I told Sandy that she would be going on to a beautiful spiritual place where there was only love. I said that her dad would take her over and she'd be with him in the spiritual realm. I feel that she was relieved. I also knew that Maureen and Lassie were both very sad. But Maureen said, *We'll be together and take care of each other. We're both pretty old and we need each other more than ever now. And please tell Lassie that when she needs to go, I want her to go back into the spirit world. She doesn't have to worry about me. She's got my permission.*

I've found that not many people think to tell that to their animals, and it really helps them to let go instead of trying to hang on because of us.

And you tell that Frank, she said, *that he'd better take as good care of her over there as he did here.*

Tell her not to worry, Frank said. *I'll do that. And you tell her to stay over there for a while because I'm not ready for her yet.*

No problem, Maureen said. *I'm not planning on leaving here anytime soon.*

Even though it was a very sad moment for everyone involved, I knew that Maureen's sense of humor would carry her through, and, in spite of Frank's teasing, I also knew that they'd have the same mutually warm and bantering relationship over there that they did on the earth plane.

Before we ended the call, Maureen said, *Thank you for your help. It was also good talking to Frank, but I wouldn't tell him that.* And I said, *Well, don't worry, darling, he can hear you anyway!*

ONE FINAL WORD

I know that not every one of these stories is going to resonate equally with every one of my readers, but I do hope that the one thing you all take away with you is the positive understanding that the animals you have loved and lost are not really lost at all. Their souls continue to exist in the spiritual realm, and because they are no longer weighed down or limited by their physical bodies, they can be with you wherever you are.

If they died of an illness or in old age, they are no longer in pain. If they died before what *you* believe should have been "their time," they are not angry or resentful. All animals, when they are on the earth plane, are much more forgiving than we humans. And when they are in spirit, they are all happy and peaceful, no matter the circumstances of their passing.

They want you to know this because they want you to be happy, as they are. Some will reincarnate during your lifetime while others will not, but in all cases, they want you to move on, not to forget them, but to give your love to another animal, because there is always more than enough love to go around.